Tales
from the end of the
Old Military Road

Stories and Tall Tales
from the
West Dalhousie Area

Revised Edition

Brenda J. Thompson

Tales from the End of the Old Military Road
© 2019 Brenda J. Thompson

Cover design: Rebekah Wetmore
Editor: Andrew Wetmore

ISBN: 978-1-998149-33-9
First edition September, 2019
Revised edition December, 2023

MOOSE HOUSE
PUBLICATIONS

2475 Perotte Road
Annapolis County, NS
B0S 1A0
moosehousepress.com
info@moosehousepress.com

We live and work in Mi'kma'ki, the ancestral and unceded territory of the Mi'kmaw people. This territory is covered by the "Treaties of Peace and Friendship" which Mi'kmaw and Wolastoqiyik (Maliseet) people first signed with the British Crown in 1725. The treaties did not deal with surrender of lands and resources but in fact recognized Mi'kmaq and Wolastoqiyik (Maliseet) title and established the rules for what was to be an ongoing relationship between nations. We are all Treaty people.

Also by Brenda J. Thompson

Enslavers of the Maritimes (2024)

A Wholesome Horror: Poor Houses in Nova Scotia

Finding Fortune: Documenting and Imagining the Life of Rose Fortune

Single Mother's Survival Guide

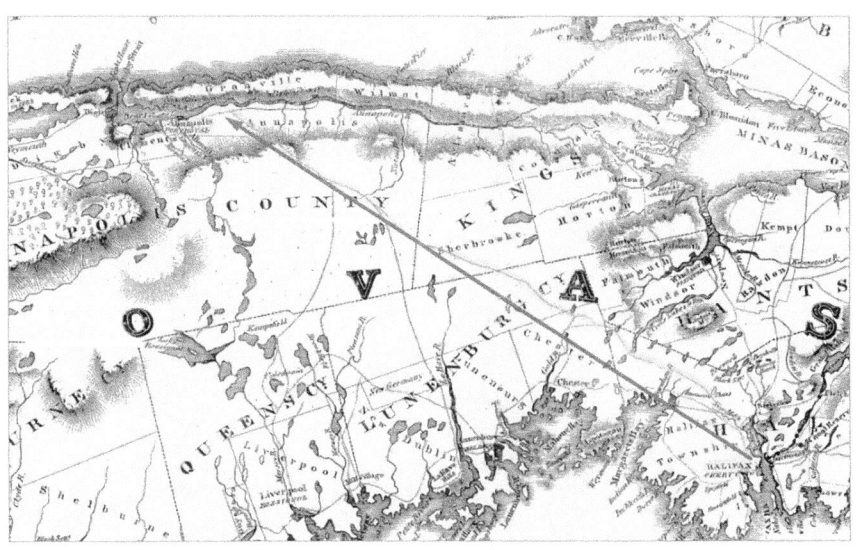

1829 map of Nova Scotia showing the length of the Military Road, from Thomas Chandler Haliburton's 'A Historical and Statistical Account of Nova Scotia', printed by Joseph Howe.

The Old Military Road

When the capital of Nova Scotia moved from Annapolis Royal, on the Bay of Fundy side of the province, to Halifax on the Atlantic side, in 1749, it was decided by the Powers That Be that a road should be built to connect the two military towns. Annapolis Royal was the gateway to the eastern United States, New Brunswick and the West Indies Construction of the road began in 1784.

The original idea was to go from Halifax to Windsor and then connect the old Acadian settlements along the Annapolis Valley and open up the interior of Nova Scotia for re-settlement by good, loyal English stock. The Napoleonic Wars interrupted the work on the roads, however. Work only resumed in 1816 with many of the settlements along its route being named after British generals. Lord Dalhousie was one of them.

One of the ways to build the road was to offer land grants to former soldiers who would, it was hoped, settle and build farms on their land. The land was not good for farming, so many of the settlers took up lumbering and milling.

Progress on the road from the Annapolis Royal end went nicely until they hit the area of Sherbrooke. We know this place today as New Ross. The numerous swamps and many large rocks made the terrain hostile to road building and the road petered out there. On the Halifax side, today, many parts of the old road are now in lakes.

The road was called the Military Road. Later the name was changed to the West Dalhousie Road. Some people, however, still referred to it as The Old Military Road.

The history of the area goes back much further than our history books tell us; back before the English settlers, back before the Acadians....

These stories are based on actual events but have been fictional-
ized. I hope you enjoy them.

BJT

To the people of Perotte, West Dalhousie, and the places nearby without a name: thank you for giving life to these communities.

Tales from the End of the Old Military Road

The Old Military Road..7
Bloody Creek...13
The Vase..17
Caves, Acadians and Paradise Lake...23
Williams, 1818..31
Why Not Both?...45
Mrs. Catherine Inglis & Mr. John Gregory......................................51
No Brag, Just Facts...70
Ernest in the Settlement...101
The Gypsies of West Dalhousie..115
Agnes and the Monsters...125

Acknowledgements...135
About the author...137

Brenda J. Thompson

Bloody Creek

It was the time before recorded time. The woods were plush with greenery, ferns, trees; and no humans were around. There were simply many reptilian-like mammals roaming around, eating leafing greens and, occasionally, each other.

The tectonic plate had been shifting over a million years, and what was once a giant land mass surrounded by ocean waters eventually separated into sections that moved further and further away from each other over the millennia. The piece of land where cradasaurous, an herbivore, now wandered had at one time shared the same red soil as the land mass that would eventually become known as West Africa.

The cradasaurous looked up from her leaf eating in curiosity. There was something in the air. Something was coming. Everything was still. There was no air movement, the birds were not flying but rather sitting in the shrubs and trees, looking up. They too sensed something was happening.

By mid-afternoon the sky had darkened. Something was blocking out the sunlight; not completely, but enough so that all creatures were looking up to the sky quizzically. Some put their heads back down and continued to eat their plants, herbs or their prey.

In the late afternoon it hit. It came in at a 15 degree angle: a monstrous ball of fire headed right toward them.

The mammals never heard it or saw it land. They were evaporated before the asteroid hit the ground.

It was the rarest form of meteorite, a low angled one, that landed on what became known later, many thousands of years later, as Bloody Creek, near the top of the South Mountain. And there were several more meteorites to hit the mountain before this period was over.

This mountain range ran from the waters of the Bay of Fundy, up the spine of the province of Nova Scotia, to fizzle out around what became known as the town of Windsor. The Mountain looked over the valley that lay between it and the North Mountains. The valley that lay in between was lush and fertile with nutrients and elements in its soil that washed down from the mountains.

Later, as scientists studied the Earth's early history, including meteorites and meteorite craters, they theorized about what had killed off the dinosaurs. At first they assumed it was a global ice age. But which ice age? There had been several of them. But what brought that global ice age on? They then theorized that the squad of meteorites that hit Earth would have caused catastrophic environmental damage. Such a series of events would have caused a dust cloud that would last for decades all over the world. This would cut down how much energy from the sun that could reach the ground, and would kill off most of the plant life. And, without the plant life, the dinosaurs would die off from lack of food.

"Where did these meteorites hit the Earth?" they asked themselves. Many studies and much research later, the scientists proclaimed that the culprit was a meteorite that had hit the peninsula of Yucatan, in what is now known as Mexico. For many years, this theory was accepted.

But some scientists weren't sure. They continued to do more research, poring over geological maps and using satellite images of the earth that were becoming available. It became clear to some scientists that the meteorites that triggered the global ice age had actually struck our planet outside where there is now a small town on a small isthmus that clings to the side of the eastern seaboard of North America.

When the meteorites hit, rocks, stones and meteorite material scattered everywhere. The meteorites dug huge divots, that eventually became lakes. Giant granite rocks were strewn around like children's toys. And many millions of years later, the scarred terrain would be named the South Mountain and groups of people would pass over it, camp and hunt on it, and, eventually, settle on it.

This place became known as West Dalhousie. And this is its story.

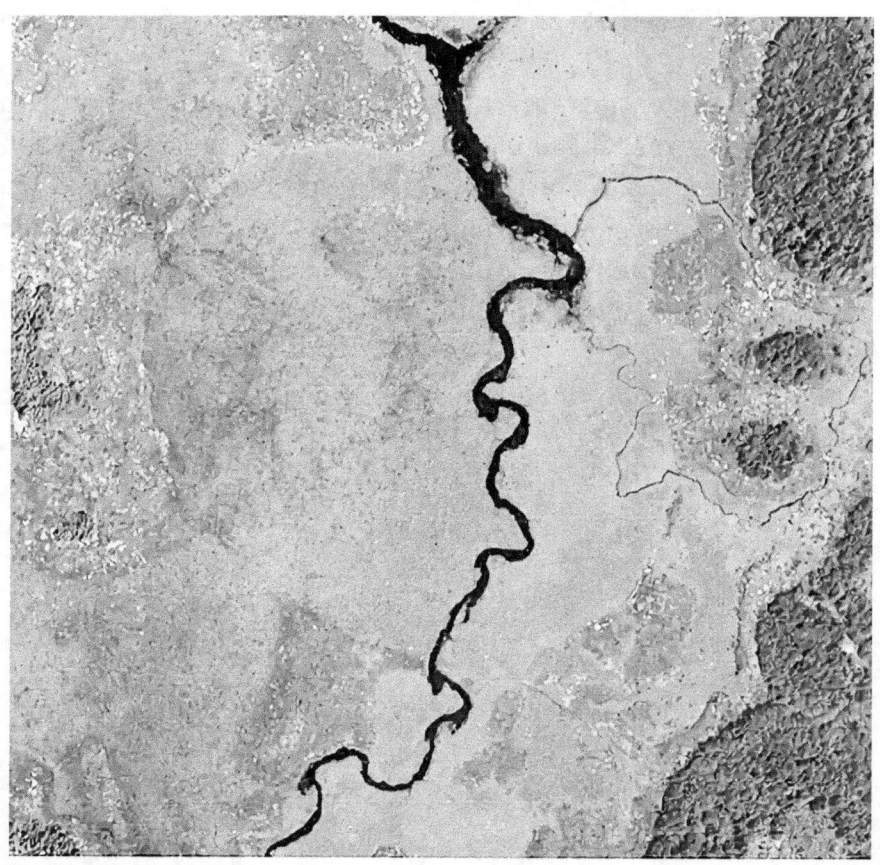

Retired Acadia University geologist George Stevens spotted an elliptical formation when viewing old aerial photographs of a site near Bridgetown, N.S. The area is now a reservoir and covered with water.

The Vase

She saw her daughter coming across the field with the men. Only, there were more men than she had expected. Some of the men looked very different from her tribesmen, from any men she had seen. Wopk, born in the morning light, knew they had visitors. She began preparing a meal.

Munkwon was tired from her travels. She had left the mountain overlooking the valley four moons ago to travel with her siblings and cousins, following the inland rivers to Pijenooiskak, where the ocean lapped up against the shore. They paddled their gwitn to a favourite island to collect acorns and berries for cooking and to hunt caribou that had swam over there. The island was known for akkada, an abundance of food.

While gathering food, they came across another group of explorers. These explorers were not of L'nu, the Mi'kmaq, nor any other of the local tribes of Wolastoqiyik, the Maliseet. Their skin was a different colour; goldish brown rather than a dark brown. Their eyes tended to point up at the outer edges, like a cat. But their hair was black and straight like L'nu and their eyes were dark and flashing as well. The new men and women were wary of the Mi'kmaq. They were on their defences, ready to be attacked.

Munkwon's eldest brother approached them first with words of greeting. "Piskwa'," he said, approaching with an open hand out and the palm up to show there was no weapon in it.

The explorers did not completely understand and stepped back.

"Piskwa'," he said again, and patted a large rock beside him. Kitpoo sat down on the rock, indicating to the group that they should sit down as well.

One of the men stepped forward. His name was Tane, he indicated. Everyone relaxed.

Through gestures and drawings in the sand, the explorers told their story of coming here from across the salt water, from a land on another sea. They had travelled on rafts and in boats made of a strange wood that repelled the water but was hollow and lightweight. They had lost several people along the way.

They drank from large seeds that had rich water in it and, when the water was gone, they could eat the inside of the seed. And then the seed could be used to carry things. They also had large leaves such as Monkwon and her people had never seen. They were big enough to cover a person's body, yet were fibrous and stringy when pulled apart. The leaf could make valuable rope.

They also carried seeds and fresh water in large clay containers that had tops on them to open the container and shut it as well. The People were fascinated.

But now the explorers needed to repair their vessels and this land had no wood such as their vessels were made from. The explorers, 21 of them in all, were trying to find some wood   to work with and food to eat. They were lucky in that they had arrived at the time of year when the wind was soft and the sun gave heat. But the winds would soon grow angry and the sun would head far up into the sky and grow cold. The snow would come and drive the people back into their caves and their birch bark wigwams.

The new people also wanted to explore this new land, to find out what it offered and who lived here. Then they wanted to take this information back to their own land.

Monkwon and her brothers and cousins spent the next moon

with these explorers. Other Mi'kmaq came and talked with the new people. Some of the new people went with the Mi'kmaq to the mainland to learn how to hunt food there and identify plants that could be eaten. They also learned how to build boats like the Mi'kmaq, with birch bark for the smaller boats and moose skins for the bigger ones.

Monkwon became friends with Akumu, one of the explorers. She found him handsome, with a warm smile. They spent time together, picking berries and learning each other's language.

After learning much about each other and through discussion, it was decided that the new people would come to the homes of Monkwan and her family, to see their community and how they lived, and stay for at least the cold season. They gathered in several moose skin canoes to travel along the coast. Before the new people left, however, they carved a message into some wood for any of their people who came behind them, to tell them what had happened and where they were.

They launched and started to follow the southern coastline on a sunny day when the cold was just beginning to show its colours in the mornings. As they paddled within site of the shoreline, they pointed out the seals, whales, porpoises, and fish of the area. The new explorers had already seen many whales and porpoises on their travels across the salt waters. At the end of each day, they caught some fish and then camped on the shoreline to eat and rest.

Eventually they came to a break in the walls of high rocks of the coast, and they steered their canoes through to a large basin of water. Mookswan told the explorers that they called this place Oositookum, because it was like an ear canal leading into the ear. Rolling hills on both sides of the water went on for as far as the eye could see.

The Mi'kmaq continued to paddle up the basin of water until it turned into a river. It was wide at first, but gradually the land came closer and closer together. When the sides of the river were very close, the Mi'kmaq stopped and pulled their canoes onto the land, ensuring the canoes were safe from the waters and ready for the next people who needed to use them. Then, carrying their goods upon their backs, they walked through the woods and up several hills until they came to an encampment on a large white rock.

It was here that Mokwan's community lived for this part of the year. They had already been down to Oositookum to fish for porpoise, which they caught and smoked and brought back to the community for eating in the harsh winter months.

Akamu and his brothers Tane and Manu were introduced to the community. Akamu, who had been carrying the large clay vessel filled with seed on his back, took it off at this point and presented it as a gift to Wokn, recognizing her as a person of importance in the village.

Tane, Manu and Akamu stayed within the Mi'kmaq village on the white rock for several moons. The snow came and the winds howled and the people gathered in wigwams for meals, stories and gossip. They learned some of the words of the explorers and the explorers learned some of their words. Both groups expressed their words in pictures, which they carved into rocks and pieces of wood.

The winds died down, the snow melted and the green came back to the earth. Tane and Manu decided it was time to leave. They were to meet their people again on the island of abundance and head back to their homeland beyond the salt water.

Akamu, however, was not leaving. He was staying here with Monkwon. She was having a baby by Akamu and he wanted to stay with this woman and her child.

They made their own wigwam on the land of white rock. Akamu went hunting and sealing with the men and Monkwon stayed and prepared for the baby. When they had a baby girl, Akamu was overjoyed. She looked so much like him! They named her Loto, for she was a piece of their hearts.

As Loto grew, she became a sister to her other siblings and their father taught them about his homeland, where he came from and some of the words from his community. He taught them how to draw pictures from his land. And he showed them the vessel that he had brought with him from the land beyond the salt water.

Loto and her siblings grew up hearing these stories and, when the time came, they passed them on to their children and grand-children. Some of the words and the stories were lost to memory along the way; some of the words and stories were changed as the oral history was passed along. But the clay vessel was kept in the village of the white rock, in a cave, to be passed along to the next generation.

After a thousand years, however, the stories became lost and the story about the clay vessel became forgotten as well. It sat in the back of a cave, forgotten about, occasionally questioned when one of the People saw it; but as there was no story to go with it, it re-mained at the back of the cave, preserved from the elements.

Brenda J. Thompson

Caves, Acadians and Paradise Lake

Marie ran as fast as her nine-year-old legs would take her. She ran through the fields with her family members: her brothers, her sisters, her father, and her mother who was clutching the baby to her breast while running. Her father had a ruck sack of food and goods over his shoulder. They had already buried the family gold under an apple tree and they all took pains to remember which tree it was. Now they were running.

It was a warm August evening last night, when their friend and Mi'kmaq neighbour, Paul Labrador, came into their home, out of breath, with news that would change their lives. "The British are taking the people," he gasped. "Word is coming from our people in Chignecto and Pizquid. The British are rounding up your people and putting them on ships to send them far away."

Marie's family was scared. They had been expecting something to happen but not this. Marie's family, one of the many Comeau families that lived outside of the British fort and town of Annapolis Royal, knew that the new British Governor Lawrence did not trust the Acadians as they had refused to pledge allegiance to the English kings for the past 44 years. But they could not pledge allegiance! If they did, the priests, instructed by Father LaLoutre, told them that they would be excommunicated and would spend the rest of their spiritual lives in purgatory. The Acadians were stuck in a political quagmire.

And now Governor Lawrence's patience with this situation was at an end. He wanted all Acadians out of the colony. He was planning to deport them south to the thirteen colonies.

Paul led the way, leading the Comeaus up the South Mountain, through swamps and lakes and around fields of enormous rocks, following a path that the Mi'kmaq had marked and only they knew. He had a place in mind, he told them, where they could hide, where his people often sheltered when they were hunting.

After two days of travelling through the woods, slowed down by babies, children, other families and the elderly people who had joined them, they came to the top of the mountain.

There were 22 of them in all. They stood at the top of the mountain on a rock that went on for acres, where no trees grew and they could see over the valley to the North Mountain.

"Come quickly," Paul motioned. He led them through the woods again, off the white bedrock and to a series of caves. "You hide here," he told them. "My brothers and sisters stay here when hunting.".

Marie peeked inside with her father. There were the remains of a cooking fire and a number of beds made of pine boughs that needed to be changed. There was also a strange looking clay vessel leaning up against the back wall of the cave. Marie looked at it carefully and then took it to her mother.

"This is good, Paul," said Claude, Marie's father. "We will stay here until we know what will happen next."

The families moved into the caves, sharing fires and food, caring for children and the elderly while the men went out hunting for moose and caribou and fished in the many lakes they were surrounded by.

They thought it would be temporary, until the end of summer. They thought that the British would come to their senses and see how much they needed the work of the Acadians to survive. After all, the Acadians were the ones who planted and harvested food for the British, showed them how to make farmland on the salty dykes of the Rivière du Dauphine. They did logging for the British and many of them had intermarried with the British. And now they were hiding out like fugitives.

The situation was not settled quickly. The snow began to fly and still Marie and her family were in the caves. It was not comfortable and they longed for the comfort of their own homes, of their straw ticks, their hearths and tables, their neighbours and friends. The cave was damp and dark. Bats regularly flew down at them while rodents shared the heat of their fires.

Paul and his brothers often came with game for food, and news of what was happening. The Grand Dérangement was happening all over the colony. Most of the Acadians had been captured and held captive in their churches until ships arrived to take them to other places. Some of the men flung themselves off the ships and swam ashore to the forest and ran. Another group of Acadians took over their ship, Paul told them, and sailed it to another part of L'Acadie. They had organized themselves into a resistance and, with the Mi'kmaq, were fighting the British.

There were other Acadians hiding in caves lower down the mountain and Paul brought two of their leaders to the upper caves. The men talked around the fire of what was to be done next. Their elderly and many of the babies had died because of the dampness in the caves. The caves were simply not suitable for long-term living and this deportation was obviously going to be a long-term situation.

They knew that British soldiers were looking for them. Paul informed them that the soldiers were regularly coming up the river, looking for signs of Acadians hiding out in the woods.

But the British did not know about these caves and, so long as no one told them, the families would be safe.

As winter subsided and spring came on, the Acadian leaders decided that they had to abandon the caves and make their own community on the shores of the lake of many rocks. Marie knew this lake, as her brothers had taken her fishing there. To Marie it looked as though someone had tossed these boulders of sandstone and quartz in the lake as you would throw pebbles. Rocks jutted up out of the water in height and size while many others were just under the surface, waiting to rip the birch from your canoe. This was why the Mi'kmaq used dugout canoes on this lake.

The lake was filled with many fish that were good to eat, and the soil near the lake was good for growing. Their Mi'kmaq friends brought them some small apple trees that they had stolen out of the earth on their former homesteads.

The Acadians planned an orchard at the look out site down the mountain. From this site, the apple trees would blend in with the forest but the workers could also see far down the river and could tell if anyone was coming. It would be a productive alarm system, this orchard.

As the Comeaus were packing up their belongings in the cave to move to the new settlement, Marie tried carrying the strange-looking clay vessel with her. It was heavy. She managed to carry it across two fields before she set it down beside a tree.

"I'll come back and get that some other day," she told herself. It's just too heavy to carry with everything else."

They laid out a settlement, choose plots of land and built traditional Acadian huts. When one of their members died, the community created a cemetery at the back of the lake in a secluded part of the settlement. After building their homes and settling in again for the winter, the community began to thrive. Young people began coupling together. Babies were conceived. Life would go on.

The next year, 1757, some British soldiers were getting too close to some of the Acadians in hiding. Watchers passed the alarm that the soldiers were moving up the river, into creeks, looking for fire-wood. Although this was nowhere near where Marie's community was, the Acadian leaders called on her father, Claude, to help defend the Acadian communities in hiding.

The British soldiers, some no older than teenage boys, were having a lark of a day. They were away from fort duties and moving their boats along the René Forêt Rivière, laughing and joking and not paying much attention as they should have been.

When the lads jumped out of their boats to start gathering fire-wood, the Acadians and Mi'kmaq attacked them, killing all but one, who managed to get away and tell the officers at Annapolis Royal.

Claude felt sick to his stomach. He had killed one of the young men himself, but he knew it had to be done to protect his family.

Several times the Acadians and the Mi'kmaq organized to attack the fort at Annapolis Royal. Several skirmishes happened and many of the British soldiers were killed, but still they could not take over the town. But neither could the British subdue the anger of the Acadians and their Mi'kmaq allies.

Some of the young Acadian men left the community, joining up with the Mi'kmaq and travelling down to the Atlantic side of the colony. There they joined up with even more angry Acadian men and the Mi'kmaq and, under the encouragement of priests such as Father LaLoutre, they attacked the foreign Protestants and the Germans in the new settlement of Lunenburg, which they knew as Mirliguèche.

The Acadians expected retaliation from the British. They prepared for it, and continued to develop their settlement on the shores of the rocky lake at the top of the South Mountain. But the soldiers did not come.

More than ten years went by. Marie's family was very settled in their home. Her father, Claude, had died just last year and was buried in the cemetery. Marie and her children often went to visit his grave.

Marie was grown up, and she and Paul's son, Thomas, who had been sweet on each other since they were small, became a couple. They married under the Catholic Church and with a Mi'kmaq ceremony. They had four children; two boys and two girls.

Their home was comfortable, with daphne shrubs planted outside and a bed cubby for Marie and Thomas inside. The children slept on straw ticks on the floor at night. Thomas was often off hunting with his brothers for extended periods of time and Marie kept the house, grew a kitchen garden, and raised the children. Marie's mother, Sophie, moved in with them when Claude died.

The summer of 1764, Thomas arrived home with some surprising news. "The hunt for Acadians is over," he told her. He had heard the news in Annapolis Royal.

Marie was shocked. She had thought the British would never give up hunting down Acadians and sending them away. Nine years of persecution and now it was over. They could come out of hiding.

The community talked about this news, deciding what to do. At first they did not trust this rumour; it was a trick the British were perpetrating on them to flush out the remaining Acadians.

But the news kept coming to their settlement from visitors and other Acadians. Some Acadian man had boldly walked down the streets of Annapolis Royal, past British soldiers, who sneered at him but did not arrest him. The rumours were true; the Grand Dérangement was over.

More discussions ensued by the shores of the rocky lake. They were free to leave. They could not go back to their old homesteads, as the British had either set them on fire and destroyed them or brought in a new bunch of people to take over the Acadian homesteads.

The British did, indeed, miss the work of the Industrious Acadians and needed to replace those they had sent away. They needed farmers to grow food, cut wood, build dykes; so they brought in a group of New Englanders who were referred to as The Planters.

Yes, the Acadians were free to go, but go where? Marie's family decided to stay where they were. They had their young family, a homestead, a comfortable life. Other families decided to leave, to try and make a better life for themselves in the towns with jobs.

Marie's sons grew up and married into the Mi'kmaq nation, raising their children in increasingly difficult situations as they were forced onto plots of land that were nothing but rocks and swamps and told to make farms there. They became known as The Metis.

One of Marie's daughters, Therese, married an Acadian man named D'entremont. They moved to the other side of the province to a place called Pubnico. Marie's other daughter, Jeanne, married a man named Buckler and stayed within the area, building their own homestead and having many children. Some survived to adulthood and lived in and around the town of Annapolis Royal.

One of the several caves in West Dalhousie where Acadians were rumoured to hide away from the British during the Grand Dérangement of 1755.

Williams, 1818

James Williams pushed his blond hair back off his face and surveyed his land grant. He listened to the sound of the men marching off through the forest til the sound of them faded away.

He thought of how excited he was when he and 86 other soldiers left Halifax on foot, marching toward their land grants and their new lives. They had drawn cards in Halifax with numbers on them to determine which soldier got which land grant.

Williams' grant was one of the last ones on this new military road that connected the ancient capital of Annapolis Royal with the new capital of Halifax. The land grant that Williams drew was on top of the South Mountain, 17 miles away from the old town of Annapolis Royal.

This was to be a reward from the government for fighting in the War of 1812. James Williams, born in Britain as a fourth son, knew that he would never inherit land in his home country. Inheritance went to the first son or the second son if the first one died. As a fourth son, he would have to make his own way in life.

His father bought him a commission in the army. It was the best he could do for a fourth son. When the opportunity came to fight in the colony of Canada, with land grants and a pension as a reward, Williams, a practical man, knew it was his best chance of ever owning land.

Twice a year, Williams was instructed, he needed to make his way into Annapolis Royal and there he would be given provisions of flour, sugar, tobacco and tea and his half pension. Hopefully, Williams thought to himself, I'll find a wife there as well.

Williams took a break from clearing brush on his land grant and looked around. He had been told the name of this place was yet to be decided but he knew it would be named after someone important. All new settlements were being named after lords and earls of England.

He was not alone here. There are a few other soldiers who had claimed their land just a few miles before his land grant. George Samson was just two miles to the west. "Although we don't get along much, I am certain we will be visiting and helping each other," Williams thought to himself. He knew that more soldiers and their families would be joining him and George Samson in the spring.

Williams was a strapping 24-year-old man. "I intend to make this here plot of land into a prosperous farm and find me a good woman to help me tend to it. I'd like to have some sons to pass this land onto and some girls to marry the local boys and have my grandchildren nearby," he thought to himself.

Williams looked around in wonder at all the land with no one on it. "I still can't believe it! After all the bloodshed, the War of 1812. They told us we would be rewarded if we helped save upper Canada from those Yanks." He chuckled out loud. "Oh we saved it, all right...we chased those Yanks right outta Canada, down into their own country and then we burned their White House down for good measure! I'll be those Yanks will never teach THAT in their history books! Yep."

He chuckled again. "I would say we soldiers earned this here reward of a land grant."

Williams picked up his axe and began chopping the branches off a fallen tree while he continued to think. "It wasn't all fun, though. I saw a lot of bloodshed, a lot of mangled bodies of soldiers from both sides. I saw a lot of things I never want to see again and wish I would stop seeing them in my dreams. They wake me up in the middle of a deep sleep many times; I have sweat running down my back and I'm screaming like I am back down there. I feel horrible every day for some of the things I have had to do."

Williams paused, looking up at the blue sky, blinking back tears. "That soldier was no more than a boy."

Williams returned to thrashing at the tree brush with a renewed vigour, trying to beat away the memories and the demons it brought with them. "But I did what I had to do. I am a man with no money. My eldest brother inherited what there was to inherit and myself and my other brothers had to go out into the world and make our own way.

"Jolly old England," he thought to himself. "If you are not born to the right family and if you are not born the right son, don't think you can just go down the road and buy some land. A simple living man like me could never afford to buy land there."

Williams moved on to whacking his axe on a white birch tree that he intended to dry and use for kindling in the winter. "Not owning land in England means you rent land from a landlord for the rest of your life. That might be acceptable for some of my brothers, but it will not be for me." The white birch fell to the ground with half a dozen good shots from his sharpened axe.

"I have no intention of giving over much of my crops, my hard earned sweat and labour, to a landlord. I would never get ahead that way. And I intend to get ahead."

Williams started gathering up some dried leaves and twigs in one spot, put some rocks around them and then lit a small fire. He put some rocks in the fire once it was going and put a gutted brook trout on one of the bigger rocks to cook it. His tin cup went beside the trout with some water and dried leaves in it. It wasn't like tea from England but it would suffice for now.

Williams thought about when he first decided to come to the new country of Upper Canada and how he ended up in the British colony of Nova Scotia. "When I heard that the government of Upper Canada would be giving out free grants of land and a lifetime pension to any man who signed up for the war against the Yanks and survived, why, I saw probably the only opportunity I would ever get to set up my own farm and start my own family. And now, finally, I have a grant of land to build my farm and family upon, to live out the rest of my life in peace and by my own labour."

Williams mused as he stirred the wood to make the fire hotter, adding more twigs and leaves. The weather in this summer month of July had not been good. There had been very little sun and hardly any warm days. Williams wondered about that as both this summer and the last summer had both been cold and sunless. Williams had already been warned that the winters in Nova Scotia could be harsh and brutal; that was why he was working every hour he could to build a shelter and put away some food and wood.

He came somewhat prepared; as prepared as he could be with his limited amount of money and what he could buy in the town of Halifax. He already had his rifle and gun powder from his brigade, and a knife and whetstone he brought from England with him. His wool blanket was also from his soldering time, though it was threadbare in some spots and had holes in others as the blanket was well used during his time sleeping in mud holes and beside boulders. He had a small coil of hemp rope, a sliver of soap, a bit of cheese and hardtack; carefully guarded in a bit of paper were some seeds for turnips, cabbage and corn. For reading, inspiration and salvation, Williams had his bible that his mother gave to him when he was a boy.

He ate his fish and drank his tea and immediately went back to work clearing trees and brush from his land. Williams did this for a few more days, but by the end of the week he was becoming concerned. He had looked all over his land and noted the size and quantity of the rocks; he noted the soil, once you got to it from taking down all the trees and stumps on it. The soil was rather thin and acidic.

"Oh, well," he told himself. "It's not what one would call 'easy farming' but I'll get a cow up here and her manure will help with making the soil better in addition to the milk she'll give me."

With these plans and dreams in mind, Williams whistled and sang quietly to himself while he worked, putting together a shelter and clearing land for a garden. Every now and then he could hear George Samson working on his land. The ring of an axe hitting a tree came up the hill some days.

Williams went down to see George occasionally, but George did not seem to want to have much to do with Williams. "It must be because of that accident with my rifle," Williams thought to himself. "I told him it was an accident. I apologized several times."

Williams outright asked George one day what his problem was. George stared at Williams like he was an idiot.

Finally, George told him. He said it was not the accident with the rifle but rather that he just didn't want anything to do with rich people.

Williams was taken aback. "Rich?" he asked. "I'm not rich. I am in the same situation as you."

George snorted with laughter and then spit his wad of chewing tobacco on the ground. "No, we are not in the same situation," he retorted. "I know what I'm doin'. You don't. Yer daddy bought you a commission with his money. And now you git a good half pension 'cause of it. I had ta earn my way through the ranks, doin' all the dirty jobs youse pretty boys didn't want to do. I cleaned up blood and guts and bodies after you rich boys sent us out to kill 'em. I stripped their dead bodies of anything useful they had on 'em and handed them over to you lot and you kept what you wanted and no sharin' with us who'd done the work. And you will git a better half pension than me even though I did all the dirt work. All because yer family is rich and mine ain't. Don't seem fair to me so I want nuthin' to do with you." George paused. "Now git."

Williams was stunned with the vehemence of George's proclamation. "But that is just the way it is, George. That is the way the Lord made it. You know that."

"I do know that," George responded. "And I don't like it. It's gonna change here in this new place 'cause I inten'ta make sure it does. Ain't no rich pretty boys gonna be my boss here in this new place."

George raised his rifle at Williams this time, aiming it at him as he said, "Now I told ya once, I'll tell ya one last time....Git! And don't come back."

Williams left, stumbling over tree stumps and rocks, and made his way back to his land grant. He had had no idea that George felt this way. He had no idea that George was smart enough to feel this way. Soldiers were just...soldiers. It was understood that they were cannon fodder for the battles, while people like him were to stay on the side lines, they were supposed to be the receivers of the glory.

Only Williams' father wasn't rich enough to purchase much glory. Williams' father, although not as rich as many other rich families in England, was just trying to protect him with purchasing him a commission. It was not his fault that he came from a better family, had more money and better connections, than George's family. "That is the way God intended it to be," Williams rationalized when thinking of George's anger.

The summer carried on with little sun. Williams worked hard, by himself, trying to make a solid shelter from the snow and rain that he knew would be coming. He could have used George's advice and help, he thought to himself.

"George is just so jealous and angry and petty that he wasn't born to a good family that I dare not ask him for anything," Williams reasoned. The memory of the rifle aimed at him rather solidified his decision not to ask George for any help.

Williams had planted his turnips, cabbage and corn seeds around the stumps that he could not get out of the earth. He cut down trees that blocked what sun there was shining on his little patch of a garden. He knew he had gotten his seeds planted late, but that couldn't be helped. His turnips were little, his cabbages were eaten by bugs and his corn grew stalks but only little unripe ears. Williams picked them anyway and put them in a hole in the ground of his shelter. This was his root cellar.

He stacked some wood up beside his shanty, made a bed of pine boughs and a chair from a stump of wood. Even though he was chastising himself for being 'luxurious', Williams made himself a small table where he could drink his tea and read his bible, like a gentleman should.

By late October the snow was lying on the ground and the wind was hissing through the treetops. An early winter was coming.

Williams could no longer hear the sound of George's axe working at clearing his land and, after a few weeks, he snuck down carefully to take a peek at George's homestead.

George had a half a shelter up, no garden, but lots of land cleared. But there was no sign of George.

Williams became bolder and walked right on to George's homestead, looking around. "Well," he chuckled to himself. "Looks like tough old George ran off and left his homestead behind. Who's the pretty boy now?"

He saw that George had left a pan behind, along with a water jug. "I deserve these," Williams said to himself while collecting up the pan and the jug, "just because he was so rude and threatening to me."

Williams noted some firewood that was still there, cut and left to season for burning next year. "He won't even be here next year. The coward done 'git'," he laughed to himself.

Williams took his six-month trip into Annapolis Royal in late November of 1815. It was a cold and long trek into the town. What made it seem really long was the huge rocks he had to climb over or get around and the many swamps he had to make his way through.

Williams did not see any other settlers or homesteads along the way. He wondered what had happened to his comrades who had also been given grants of land. "Why didn't they settle down?" he asked himself. "I guess I'm the only one tough enough to do the work and become a successful farmer."

Williams collected his half pension and heard the news that a depot for paying out pensions and buying necessities would be built up on the high hill by Clear Lake at the end of next year. They were calling it Dargie's Hill, after the businessman Chas. Dargie.

"That is good news," he thought to himself. Then he wouldn't have to come all the way into the old capital to buy provisions.

But Williams didn't mind Annapolis Royal. He bought some flour, cheese, salt, molasses and matches for his shanty. He took to the local tavern down by the wharves, listened to the men talk and looked around at the women. There were several fine and sturdy looking women around the town and in the tavern.

Williams didn't want any fancy lady; they couldn't survive on a homestead. He wanted a woman who knew how to work a farm, have healthy babies and go right back to milking the cows. He wanted a woman for baking, and cooking and, if needed, plowing the fields.

"Delicate women were best for mistresses," he told himself. Least, that was what his daddy told him when he left for Canada.

Williams made his way back to his homestead and prepared to

settle in for the duration of the winter. At first, it wasn't too bad. Williams whittled away at wood, making spoons, forks, and axe handles while the light was still good. He read the bible out loud to himself every day to remind himself of what the good Lord would provide to him if he behaved himself.

But the whittling got boring; it gave him time to think. And Williams thought a lot that winter. He thought about the home he had left behind, and the comfort of his bed, his brothers and sisters and his mother. He thought of the manners there, where people knew their place and didn't speak to him such as George had.

"People here in this colony think like republicans," he growled to himself.

On the good days when there was some sun, Williams got out and set some rabbit snares or tried to catch some fish in the freezing brook that ran through his land grant.

And then the snow hit.

It hit just before Christmas. Williams woke up one night on his bed made of pine boughs and listened to the wind blow like a fury. It shook and rattled his shanty and Williams instantly wished he had made it a bit sturdier.

He waited until the light came in through the smoke hole in the roof and then got up and stoked up his fire. The green wood just would not give off heat and the smoke collected in his shanty as the wind blew it back down the smoke hole. Williams coughed and coughed, his eyes were burning and stinging.

Eventually he gave up on the fire and crawled under his blanket and shivered until he fell asleep. When he woke up again, it was dark but the wind had died down.

Williams was ravenous with hunger and groped around in the dark to make a fire. He got a fire going and put his tin cup on the rock in the middle to melt the snow inside it and make some tea.

With the light now showing his way, Williams opened the door to get some wood from outside. He was met with a wall of snow that went up to his waistline.

Williams closed the door and tried not to panic. He had been through snowstorms before in Upper Canada. But he had never seen snow accumulate like this, so fast, so high.

He put on his army boots, which didn't give much protection against the cold, and opened the door to start digging his way out. He used his hands until they were numb from the snow, then he closed the door and wrapped his hands around his tin cup of tea. When his hands warmed up, he went back to shovelling the snow with his hands. Eventually he had made a path leading to his wood. He brought some into the hut, hoping to thaw the wood out for a fire.

Williams sat around his sputtering fire, trying to coax it into a bigger blaze so that he could cook his turnips and his unripened ears of corn. But the fire merely sputtered, staying small and cold, providing him only with a bit of light for the many hours of darkness that winter on this god-forsaken hill brought him.

It was impossible to read the small print in his bible now. Instead Williams huddled around his fire, ripping off pieces of hardtack and hardened, mouldy cheese and drinking hot water from snow he had melted. There wasn't enough room to walk around his shanty. His bed of boughs took up one whole wall, the root cellar took up one corner and his chair and table took up the other corner.

The snow continued to fall, the winds continued to howl, the days remained dark and the wood refused to burn or give heat. By the end of January, Williams was rationing his wood and his food and was using pages from his bible to start his fires or keep them going. He figured the Lord would understand.

He talked aloud to himself, trying to keep from going insane with loneliness. He was the only human on this hill, he thought.

And now he understood why.

The days passed so slowly, mostly in darkness and cold. Williams spent most of his time lying on his bed of boughs, reaching out occasionally to stoke the feeble fire, drink some tea or hot water, and nibble on frozen turnips or corn ears.

By February the light was staying longer, but the snow continued to fall and the winds continued to howl. Williams began to make plans for escaping this hell once a thaw hit. But every day he thought it would be okay to escape, he could only make it so far when either the snow started again or he was blocked by snow drifts and couldn't tell which way he was going.

By March, 1818, Williams was almost out of food. He tried hunting for moose or caribou or even rabbits, but they always outsmarted him and he wasted his gunpowder. The men of his regiment would always do this work when they were in Upper Canada so Williams did not have the experience in tracking animals for prey.

At the end of March, Williams was weak with hunger. His muscles had gone soft from lying in his bed most days, shivering and trying to keep warm. But he saw his chance to escape.

Wrapping his blanket around him, taking what little food he had and his empty rifle, Williams made his way down the trail that he could now see with the snow being much lower now. He followed it among the boulders and around the swamps and lakes for many hours until he eventually came into Lequille.

There he collapsed and the good people of the hamlet rescued him, putting him in a warm bed and spoon feeding him broth until he felt better. Once he had recovered a bit, Williams immediately found a room to rent in the town of Annapolis Royal.

April 15, 1818, George Samson and his wife and children arrived at their homestead in Dalhousie. He immediately commenced finishing his shelter and planting the seeds he had brought with him. He wanted to have a large crop this year.

George had also brought a cow and two goats, and the sound of their bells ringing whenever they moved warmed his heart. His children played around the homestead and his wife set to cooking up meals and washing laundry that flapped in the spring breeze.

George sighed with contentment. He knew more settlers were just behind him and would arrive any day to claim their homestead and begin building a community.

Eventually George got to wondering about James Williams and if he survived the winter up here. "Damn fool should have moved into town for the winter and come back in the spring like I did."

Eventually George went looking for Williams at his homestead. Just like Williams had done a few months ago, George sneaked around Williams' homestead, being careful not to be seen. He became bolder as he realized that either Williams was dead in the shelter or not there at all.

George went into the shelter and saw that it was empty; no body of Williams frozen to death. He recognized his pan and his jug and immediately picked them up, reclaiming them.

"So, Williams, I guess you took my advice and you done git," he chuckled to himself as he returned to his family homestead to greet the new settlers just arriving.

The village of Dalhousie did not see Williams again for fifty years. Williams lived in Annapolis Royal, became a moderately successful merchant, married and had children. But his memory of the winter of 1817 on the god-forsaken hill of Dalhousie stayed forever in his nightmares, replacing the ones of war and killing.

Williams only returned to Dalhousie when a local historian asked him to come with him and identify where he had lived that winter. Williams found the small root cellar he had dug and the stones around his fire pit. His shelter was gone, his garden was reclaimed by trees. He shuddered at the memories of being here.

"Why on earth did you want me to come up here and show you

where I lived that winter?" Williams asked. "Why would you want me to relive those memories?"

"You may not have stayed here more than the winter," said the young whipper-snapper of a history writer, "but you are the first settler of Dalhousie. The other settlers came just two weeks after you left."

"Two more weeks," Williams thought to himself. "If I had stayed just two more weeks, how different would my life have been? Would I have had a farm? An estate? Would I have become a leader of the community? Would I have made more money?"

He shrugged his shoulders and turned away, back to the life he had chosen.

Brenda J. Thompson

Why Not Both?

Lord Dalhousie looked down from atop his bay horse at the dark-skinned farmer. Children were standing around staring up at him, not paying any attention to the cold rain falling on them.

The 'farm' was nothing more than a shanty with a few chickens running around and a small patch of turned soil that looked like nothing more than rocks and mud on this clouded-over, cold, late-November day.

Dalhousie, dressed in his wool greatcoat with his military hat designating his status, could see more shanties beyond the farm. Several Africans were working in the rain, and stopped as they noticed Dalhousie and his fellow travellers.

Dalhousie and men had stumbled upon a community of Africans located deep in the woods of the South Mountain. He had heard of Africans leaving the white towns, making communities in the woods for themselves, but this was the first time he had actually seen one himself.

The man of the house, the farmer, moved toward him in greetings. "Welcome, Suh," he said. "Welcome to our humble farm, our community. Can we offer you a drink or some victuals? We ain't got much but what we has, we share."

Dalhousie looked with disgust at the shanty. He certainly wasn't eating there.

He turned to the Anglican bishop, Dr. Inglis, and to the other gentlemen who were travelling with him. They looked as appalled at the idea as Dalhousie felt.

"Thank you for the delightful offer," he drawled with his British accent, emphasizing the word 'delightful' with sarcasm, "But we must be moving on to reach our inn by nightfall."

The men on horseback moved as if to draw their horses away and move along the rocky path on the mountain, when the farmer spoke again

"You all must be the bunch from Lord Dalhousie. We heard he was comin' this way someday soon. We ain't never seen a bunch of gentlemen such as yerselves around here, so you must be them."

Lord Dalhousie turned in his saddle to look again at the farmer. "Yes," he drawled." I am Lord Dalhousie. I am here to inspect this part of the colony. And who might you be?"

The farmer extended his hand in greeting, which Lord Dalhousie ignored. "I'm James Moses," he said with obvious pride. "And this is my family and my farm and my community." He put his hand back down.

"Good heavens," Dalhousie thought to himself. "He is actually proud of this place."

"Tell me, Mr. Moses," he asked aloud, "what do you people grow here on your 'farm'? Rocks, perhaps?"

The other gentlemen on horseback sniggered, but Moses ignored them. "Mostly I grow turnips, potatoes, corn. Anything to get us through the winter. I trade with neighbours for things like wood for heat. We all got together and bought us a goat. The milk is shared amongst all us Africans."

Dalhousie sighed. "How can you live like this, man?" he demanded. "How can you make your woman and your children live like this? Your children are barely clothed; you and your woman look half starved. This is a cold, muddy country and you and the other negroes cannot be used to this. You Africans are used to a warm climate down south where your masters are."

Moses looked hurt but put his chest out proudly. "We are gonna get used to this because this is our farm. We made this our place, our community, with our sweat and labour. We can grow whatever we want, eat what we grow and sell the rest. This is our community."

Dalhousie muttered, "Yes, and I can see the results for myself." Then looking back at Moses, he said in a normal tone, "Wouldn't you prefer to return to the South? Yes, you were slaves; but you were kept warm, you were fed, you did not have to worry about trying to feed your children. The crops grow there all year around, but here..."he made a sweeping gesture with his arm "....here, there is only a short time to grow food. You and your family are cold and living in terrible conditions. Wouldn't you prefer to return to your master, if he would have you?"

Moses looked both terrified and angry. "No, suh," he said. "No, sur. I would not want to move myself and my family back to my old master. Master Bradley, he was handy with the whip. He was handy with the auctions if he wanted to sell one of us off. He was handy with taking the food away from us if he don't like how we were acting. No, suh," Moses repeated. "It may be cold here; the white people still might not treat us very well. We may go hungry at times, but we are free here. No one owns us here."

"You are free, all right," Dalhousie retorted. "You are free to freeze, to starve, to die alone on this rock patch you call your farm. I would think you and your people would be grateful to return to your southern masters if they would accept you back. I have no intention of recommending any help for you and your people unless you will return. You are signing your own death warrants by staying here. Good day, sir."

With that, Dalhousie and his travelling companions turned their magnificent horses away from the Moses family and trotted down the narrow path on the South Mountain towards Annapolis Royal.

Moses and the community were frightened. Was this lord going to make them all go back to their masters in the south? Some of them declared they would kill their families and themselves before they would go. Moses told them to hush with that talk, as suicide was a sin.

That night, around the fire in one of the huts, the men discussed breaking up the community and moving to someplace else. They couldn't risk that lord telling more white men in power just where they were when it came time to round them all up and send them back to their masters. That lord, just like other white people, refused to accept the fact that they were poor because of the awful way many of the white people treated them.

Later that evening, as they supped in the tavern in the township of Annapolis Royal, Dalhousie discussed this conversation with his companions. "I believe the former slaves would be better off if we could send them back to the American colonies," he said. "They are sick here and starving. They work for less pay than white men and that is causing a problem in Halifax and Shelburne. White men are starving, too, but won't, can't, work for the wages that a black man will take."

His companions muttered in agreement while eating meat and drinking spirits. One suggested, "They are a burden on our society as well. There are so many of them needin' rations. We got enough white people needing rations; we don't need Africans wanting rations, too. Have you seen how many of the negroes are in the Halifax Poor House? Why, some of the negroes purposely commit crimes, hoping to get caught, so they can lounge around in the prison for the winter, getting a warm blanket and some meals. Such a drain on the good taxpayers of this country."

The others nodded, ignoring the fact that many white paupers did exactly the same thing.

Dalhousie slapped his hand down hard on the wooden table.

"That does it," he said. "I've made up my mind. When I get back to Halifax, I am going to speak with my gentlemen friends in the government and see if we cannot make arrangements with the masters in the south to take their negroes back. That way we won't have to support them and have them take our jobs away. It will be good for the negroes, too. They won't be so cold and hungry down there like they are up here."

The men raised their mugs in agreement, toasting the idea. Lord Dalhousie was so brilliant, they decided.

"Here's to Lord Dalhousie," declared Dr. Inglis. "We should name one of the new settlements or the new schools after you."

The men raised their mugs in agreement again.

"Why not both?" Lord Dalhousie asked.

The men all laughed and agreed that this was a good idea.

And so it happened.

Racist Letter from Lord Dalhousie to the Earl of Bathurst,1816. Last paragraph on this page: "Permit me to state plainly to your Lordship that little hope can be entertained of settling these people so as to provide for their families and, wants. They must be supported for many years. Slaves by habit & education, no longer working under the dread..." The second page continues: "...of the lash. Their idea of freedom is idleness and they are, therefore, quite incapable of industry."

Eight months later, Lord Dalhousie visited many of the "Free Black Settlements" and changed his mind about sending them back to their masters in the US. Dalhousie was impressed by the industriousness of the people of the communities. From the Nova Scotia Archives.

Mrs. Catherine Inglis & Mr. John Gregory

I liked him at first. He seemed to be a bit of a lost soul. No family around him, no wife and no children. Just him. He set up his cobbler business, and heaven knows we needed a cobbler, but he did not seem to take to anyone.

Prior to the arrival of John Gregory, the cobbler, we had to take our shoes and boots to the shoemaker in Dalhousie Settlement. Dalhousie Settlement is not that far away from our home in Ramsay Township, but it still took a lot of time out of your day to go walk there, drop off your footwear that needed repairin' and then walk home again, only to turn around the next week, walk to the settlement, pick up your boots, and walk back again.

People around here are busy. The men are farmin' and loggin' and we women are working in our kitchen gardens, keepin' the fire going at all times...and that is just some of the things we are doing. So we don't have a lot of time to go to Dalhousie unless it's for church. But me and my family, we go to the church in Clear Lake, in the other direction, heading toward the old capital of Annapolis Royal.

As I said, I liked him at first. He seemed kinda lonely... and bewildered when all the young single maids came around with their pretty boots that didn't need fixin'. They were just wantin' to git to know this young man, John Gregory, and see why he didn't have a wife and did he want one?

My husband, Samuel, brought him home for supper one night, trying to bring him into the fold of the township. My, but John Gregory ate and ate! He was like a starving man. He smiled and talked and ate some more. He enjoyed everything I put in front of him with a big smile and a "Thank You, Ma'am!!"

My two children that are still here at home with Samuel and me were wide-eyed with amazement at how much John Gregory opened up and smiled and talked. Oh how we enjoyed John Gregory's company, his stories, those first few months.

~

I moved to Ramsay settlement trying to escape my memories, my past that keeps haunting me. I hoped it would not follow me here to this new place.

I had heard from people in Mud Creek that this township needed a cobbler and as that is my trade and I don't know anyone who lives up there on the top of the mountain, I decided to make my way there.

At first I had decided to just keep to myself. Keep my mouth closed and my head down and work. That was to be my life, I decided.

These silly young fillies kept coming around with their best boots, trying to tell me they needed fixing when they did not. I refused to pretend to fix them. I sent them home with their boots and told them to keep their money. I knew they just wanted to figure out who the new man in the township was. Why, they were even coming from Dalhousie, and that settlement already had a cobbler.

The fact that I wouldn't pretend to fix their boots and charge them money seemed to put me in good stead with the township. I liked that. I just wanted to make my way in life, quietly and with no more goings-on. I'd had enough of gossip and intrigues.

Then Samuel Inglis came around one autumn day, invited me to come and take victuals with him and his family. Why, I was delighted at the idea.

Inglis and his wife and children were all sitting at the kitchen table, wide-eyed at this stranger. I was asked questions and I answered them as best I could, avoiding those answers I did not want to give.

I told them stories about my days growing up on the streets of Halifax as an orphan that kept running away from the orphanage. I told them how I was drawn to the ships in the harbour and the sailors who spoke with strange words and accents, whose ships brought supplies that smelled like things that come to you in a dream. But it was rough down by the ships; the men were rough and the women were rougher.

By this time Mrs. Inglis was giving me looks with her eyes to mind my stories with the children present. I abided and told stories about travelling by ship down to Cape Sable and how rough the sea was, how the area was a lot of wind-blown trees and large rocks with fishing shacks spread all over the area. But being on a ship with all its motions made me sick and I knew I was not going to survive as a sailor.

I told them how I went back to Halifax and finally gave in to the orphanage. By this time I was old enough to be an apprentice, so they set me up with a shoemaker in Halifax. That shoemaker, he was rough on me. I slept in the barn with the animals and he gave me so little to eat that sometimes I stole the food from the cows and pigs.

I was never permitted to come into the shoemaker's house, for he had daughters and he intended them to be married to some government clerks or some such thing. He wanted them to marry up and into a better class and I was to stay away from them no matter what. So I slept in the barn, stole food from the cattle and grew up learning how to make and repair boots and shoes, working every hour that I wasn't sleeping.

By the time I reached the age of 16, one of the daughters had noticed me and the shoemaker announced that my apprenticeship was over and I was out on the street again by myself with no tools, no clothes and no money.

Mr. and Mrs. Inglis were riveted by my stories. They asked all sorts of questions. Some I answered honestly. Some I lied about.

Eventually, I was over to the Inglis' house for supper at least once a week. I lived for those suppers. It made me feel like I was finally belonging to a family. Good food, laughter, telling and listening.

The children even started calling me Uncle John. The older children who were married brought their children over and I got to bounce them on my knees. It was everything I had ever wanted.

But it didn't last. It never does.

~

Oh, we enjoyed the company of John Gregory so much those first few months. He loved my grandbabies and he enjoyed our company, as well.

At first he made shoes for my children and brought them over. He refused to take pay for them. He said our meals and family were enough pay for him.

My children loved their shoes; they were fancy with shiny buckles and patterns on the leather. They started calling him Uncle John.

The townspeople started to laugh, saying that John Gregory was at our house so much that he was starting to look like a member of the family. I could not understand, though, why he would not take up with any of the local maidens. There were enough of them around that he could have had his pick and made his own family, just like ours.

One time when John Gregory and I were alone for a few moments in the kitchen, I got nosy and asked him why he didn't start courting one of the local girls. He was into his 30s; well past time to settle down and start a family.

He just shrugged his shoulders and smiled shyly at me, said he just hadn't found the right one.

I told him how Samuel and I met and how grateful I was that he married me. My life over on the shore of the Fundy had not been very easy. I skirted around giving too much information about living there and said nothing about my time in Halifax. No one except me and Samuel needed to know that.

After John Gregory made shoes for the children, he made a pair of beautiful boots for Samuel. Samuel insisted on paying him, but John Gregory refused to take money. He asked that we just keep him in the family. We laughingly agreed that he was now a family member.

Then John Gregory presented me with a pair of lady's boots such as I had never seen. They were beautiful. So beautiful I knew I would never wear them in the backwoods of this settlement. I could not wear them to church or I would be accused of being vain.

Oh, but they were something, these boots. John Gregory had bleached the leather to white, had put four silver buckles all the way up the shin of the boot with ribbons for laces. He had tooled in patterns of flowers and hearts along the toes of the boots and put a princess heel on the back. These lady's boots were fit for royalty. And I was just a hard-working woman in my 50s in the backwoods of Nova Scotia.

As I was stunned by the boots, Samuel was taken aback. His eyebrows were raised in questions.

Later that evening when we were in bed, we talked about John Gregory's gift to me. "Them boots seem kind of intimate," Samuel said. "I dunno. I'm thinking he has a yen for you."

"Don't be silly, husband," I laughed. "I'm old enough to be his mother."

"That ain't enough to stop some men," he snorted. Then he rolled over and went to sleep.

Things changed after that day. Samuel was keeping an eye on John Gregory and his "intentions". Me? Well I was rather flattered that John Gregory would see me in that way, but I knew the whole thing was silly. I was 51 years old, a grandmother, married for many years. I had wrinkles and grey hair. Why on earth would a young man like John Gregory be interested in me?

~

Catherine loved the boots. I had stopped calling her Mrs. Inglis by now and called her by her Christian name as I was now a member of their family. They had told me so one evening after I gave Samuel the boots I had made for him.

I worked long and hard on Catherine's boots. I saved up some money and sent away to Halifax for the buckles and ribbons. I wanted these boots to be very special to her. I wanted to know that every time she looked at those boots, put on those boots, she would smile and think of me. I worked carefully on the hearts and flowers that I tooled into the soft white leather. I thought of how she should have something special, just like her, to show her that she was a special person.

When I presented the boots, Catherine was stunned by the beauty of them and the work that went into them, the buckles and the ribbons. Samuel, however, did not look entirely pleased. His eyebrows were up and he looked questioningly at me. I smiled back him and told him how lucky he was to have Catherine as his wife.

~

John Gregory continued to come over for supper, but now it was just once in awhile. Samuel started putting John Gregory off from joining our family at meal times or at any time. I was sad about that because I missed John Gregory's stories, but I knew that if a young woman had given a gift like those boots to Samuel, I would be hoppin' mad and would throw that filly in the brook.

John Gregory seemed confused by Samuel's distance and tried even harder to please us. When he showed up with a second pair of lady's boots for me, Samuel had had enough. The invitations for supper stopped completely.

Samuel got together with a couple of his friends and they went over to John Gregory's cobbler shop one evening to "have a talk."

Samuel told John Gregory, "You need to stay away from my wife".

John Gregory said, "I'm not interested in her that way. Why do you think I want her that way?"

One of Samuel's friends said, "She is old enough to be your mother, John Gregory."

"I know," John Gregory said. "And that is why I don't want her that way. I want to be with her for just the person she is.".

"Well, that's not going to happen any more," Samuel said. "Those boots you made her, well, they are just too"—he searched for the word—"they were made with too much passion. I see how you look at my wife and I am telling you now, in front of these here witnesses, stay away from her. Or you'll have us to deal with."

John Gregory stayed away after that. For a while I missed him. But then I would see him, from a distance, watching me, staring at me. And it made me uncomfortable.

That look was familiar to me. At first he looked at me with sadness in his eyes. Then his expression started turning to anger. I began avoiding any place where John Gregory might be. I avoided looking at him when I did see him. Samuel and I began to talk of moving to Dalhousie.

~

I could not believe what Samuel and these men were saying to me. All I had tried to do was be nice to Samuel's family, to show my gratitude for bringing me into the family. I tried to make sure that Catherine (Samuel stopped me here in my explanation and said, "You shall call her Mrs. Inglis from now on") had whatever nice things I could give her.

All I had done was shown this family love through my gifts. I saw all that Catherine did for her family; I saw what she said and how she said it. I saw the features on her face, her expressions, her laughter and I felt at home with her.

"Stay away from her," I was told. "Stay away from her and all of my family," Samuel Inglis told me.

So I did. At first. I missed the suppers so much, I missed the family. But mostly I missed Catherine. Each time I saw her in the township, I felt such sadness. I felt she missed me, too, and I tried to show her that each time I saw her.

Then Samuel caught me one day, looking over at Catherine. Catherine had not even seen me, but Samuel caught me looking at her and missing her. He grabbed me roughly and pulled me in behind one of the buildings.

"Don't you ever look at my wife again," he told me.

"You can't stop me," I retorted back to him. "Looking ain't a crime.".

"Well, she thinks you are nothing but a sad, silly little man,"

Samuel told me. "She laughs at you when we talk together about you. She laughs at those silly booties you gave her. Every time she looks at them, she laughs at you. What were you thinking, giving foolish boots like those to a woman who is old enough to be your mother?"

I pushed Samuel off me. I was so hurt I could feel the tears coming. I did not want to cry in front of him so I pushed him off me and I walked away. I walked to my shop and shut the door. And I cried like a little boy. I couldn't help it.

The tears just came and came and for two days, I didn't answer the door, I didn't fix any boots or shoes, I just lied in my bed and thought about what Samuel had said to me and cried some more.

Finally I pulled myself together and opened my shop door again. People were not coming to me like they used to. They had heard the rumours about Catherine and me and they were staying away. It was just like before. I thought I had left all that but this was worse than ever.

Through the winter I just kept my head down and my hands busy as I worked. The words that Samuel had said to me that day were stuck in my head and wouldn't go away. "Foolish little man." "Laughs at you every time she looks at those boots."

The words looped around in my head, again and again and again. Every time I managed to make them go away for a bit, I saw Catherine and she saw me. And the words came back to mock me again. I became very angry about those words. I became very angry at her.

~

I had some grain left but it needed to be ground into flour. It was a long walk down the old military road to the grist mill in the community of Lequille but I decided to pick a day at the beginning of the summer. Late in June I got up early one morning and, telling Samuel I was going to the grist mill and that I would be home late in the evening, I took a basket of eggs and butter for trading, my birch cup for drinking, some bread and cheese for eating, and my sack of grain for grinding into flour.

The sun came up within the hour and I knew I had picked a good day for this trip. If there was a lineup at the grist mill and I was late getting home, I knew the moon would be full tonight and it would help guide me up the military road to the Township.

I passed several homesteads and farms along the way, crossed the stone bridge over the stillwater by the Buckler Inn, passed the saw mill just past the Inn, and waved to Mrs. Ramsay at her estate. She and her husband, Colonel Ramsay, had a beautiful big farm just outside the new settlement of Perotte. My township had been named after one of his relatives, Lord Dalhousie's son, nearly 20 years ago.

I skirted the lakes and swamps, traversed the hills and finally walked into the hamlet of Lequille. Arriving at the grist mill, I marked my place in the lineup and then went up the hill to trade my eggs and butter at the local general store. They gave me some credit and I bought some things we needed at home, like molasses and tea.

By the time I got back to the grist mill, someone had already taken my grain and ground it into a fine flour. That was quite neighbourly of them to do that. I paid for the grinding and got on my way. If I walked quickly enough, I might make it to Mrs. Todd's for tea at Lake LaRose.

I was getting tired by the time I arrived at Mrs. Todd's but she was gracious enough to let me sit and down and put my dusty feet up while she made me tea and let me eat my bread and cheese.

We talked about local events, who was marrying who, who had died, who was dying, who was having a baby...that kind of stuff. I loved drinking tea and finding out what was happening in other communities. It warmed my heart and refreshed me and I was on my way again, feeling better.

By the time I got to the turn-off to the Perotte Settlement, I was beginning to feel thirsty. I knew there was a good fresh-water stream up ahead and I aimed my walk for it.

As I came up over the hill, I saw a man standing there, leaning up against one of the big rocks, carving on an apple stave. He looked up at me and smiled. It was John Gregory.

~

I saw Catherine leave early that morning. I couldn't sleep. Those words were in my head, whirling around and hurting me again. When I saw Catherine quietly walk by with a sack of grain and a basket of eggs and butter, I knew where she was going. I quickly gathered some gear and began to follow her. I needed to talk to her. I needed to find out if she really said those words that hurt me so much.

I watched her walking past the farms and homesteads; I watched her cross the stone bridge by the Buckler Inn, I saw her wave to Colonel Ramsay's wife. I tried to catch up with her by the lakes but she was moving very quickly and there was no place for a private conversation, I knew, between the lakes and Lequille.

So I decided to wait for her when she came back. I made myself comfortable by the big boulder atop the hill that marked the road into the Perotte Settlement. I knew she would be a few hours yet, but I was patient.

I watched the sun move across the sky, listened to the birds chattering with each other and the squirrels nattering away, warning others about my presence. I saw a moose lumber through the woods at a distance, but I kept still and made no noise.

When the sun began to dip down beneath its zenith, I pulled an apple stave out of my gear and began carving it with my knife. I may as well make use of my time, sitting here waiting, and do up some apple staves that I needed in my shop.

Eventually I wandered to the top of the next hill and I could see, down the military road by Lake LaRose, that Catherine was on her way back. I ran back to the boulder and positioned myself so that she would see me at the last minute and couldn't avoid me.

When Catherine came atop the hill and saw me, she was surprised at first. And then frightened. I could see it in her eyes. I approached her in a friendly manner, saying Hello, that I hadn't talked to her in a long time and that I missed her. I was hoping she would respond by telling me that she missed me, too.

Instead she responded with anger. "Didn't my husband tell you to stay away from me?" she spat out.

I was taken aback. "He did," I told her. "He told me some other things as well. I don't know why he told me these things. I am sure they are not true."

Catherine was rummaging in her basket and pulled out her birch cup. She walked toward the freshwater stream.

"Are you calling my husband a liar?" she snapped.

"No, no I am not. I just think he misunderstood what you were saying and then repeated it to me."

Catherine got herself a drink from the stream and stood up to face me. "We gave you love, John Gregory. We brought you into our family. We treated you as one of our own. And in return you want my husband's wife?"

"No," I said. "It isn't like that."

Catherine sighed with resignation. She looked like she had something to say that she didn't want to say, but that I was forcing her into it.

"I know what you know, John Gregory," she said. "I know it, too. I figured it out. And I want you to know I will never accept you that way. Never. So you'd best just leave it and go away. Because if you don't go away, Samuel and I are fetchin' on leaving ourselves. And all because of you."

I swore at court that he didn't know what happened next. The trees seemed to swirl around me, a curtain of filmy red dropped before my eyes. I felt like I could see over the treetops, I was lifted so high. I felt my strength match that of a team of oxen, my arms and legs were exploding with power...and rage.

~

I saw John Gregory standing there, carving an apple stave. I was surprised...and then frightened. "When Samuel hears about this, he's gonna beat him," I thought. "And he'll go to gaol for it. I have to just get rid of him for once and for all, make sure he never approaches me again."

John Gregory was all friendly to me, not angry-looking like had been for the past month or so. I reminded him that my husband would not be happy to know that he was here, waiting for me, when Samuel had already warned him off of me.

John Gregory just said he wanted to talk with me; he said that Samuel had said some things to him, said that I had said those things, and he just felt they weren't true. I didn't know just what Samuel had said to him but I wanted John Gregory to go away.

"You calling my husband a liar?" I snapped at him.

"No, no," he said obsequiously, like a snivelling weasel. "I just figured he misunderstood what you said and then told me. I know you wouldn't say things like that about me."

I bent down and got my drink from the stream. I needed time to think. I needed to get rid of John Gregory forever.

I decided to take the chance. "Look, John Gregory," I told him. "I know what you know because I figured it out myself. And I want you to know that I will never accept you that way. Never."

I went on to tell him that either he had to move or Samuel and I would move but I don't' think he heard me because his face went white and kind of shocked looking. His eyes actually rolled back in his head.

The next thing I knew I was on the ground of the forest and it was night. It was dark and quiet. I was in so much pain...so much pain in my head and chest. I tried to move and I groaned a little. And there was John Gregory, standing over me. I could see his face even though it was pitch black. I softly pleaded with him.

"No" was the last word I ever uttered.

~

I got back to my cobbler's shop late at night. I pulled the blankets right up over my head but my eyes were wide open. The words had stopped swirling in my head, finally. Instead, flashes of rage and blood and flesh kept exploding in my head. I watched them, eyes wide open, under my blankets in the dark, over and over again.

And then a question arose in my head in the midst of those flashes. Was I finished? Was it done? The two questions took the place of the flashes in my head to the point where I got up and sneaked off again, back down the old military road. I moved as quickly as I could in the dark, miles and miles down the road until I got to the stream just past the Ramsay estate.

There it was, bloodied, lying there by the stream. I checked to see if I was finished. It groaned weakly. I was not finished. I picked up a huge rock and held it over my head. It opened its eyes and looked right into mine.

"No," was all it said before I brought the rock down on its face. I was finished.

I knew that the township people would eventually come looking for it so I dragged it over behind a large tree that had been felled by the wind. I left it there. I was finished. It was over.

I felt exhausted. Exhausted beyond this life. I was tired of everything. I was tired from all the miles walked; I was tired from the lies; I was tired of what I had done; I was tired of this life.

I tried to sneak into the Ramsay barn to sleep for a few hours before heading back to the township, but his dogs alerted him to me. Colonel Ramsay came out to the barn and saw me and said it was all right if I slept there, but I was to make my way at first light.

I was back down the old military road before the sun came up and back at my shop as the township was stirring awake.

By mid afternoon I was shaking with exhaustion and sickness. I saw Samuel Inglis walking around, talking to the women, asking them if they had seen Catherine. All of them shook their heads. At one point, Samuel looked over at me. I thought he was going to speak to me but instead he gave me a hard look and walked away.

I slept that night but woke up screaming. I dreamt again of blood and flesh and rocks and apple staves stabbing flesh. I dreamt of it laughing at me as I hit it again and again and again with the rock.

By the next morning Samuel was organizing a search party to go looking for Catherine. People of the township were putting down their farming tools and taking off their aprons and joining in the search party. I joined as well. It would have looked bad if I didn't.

I kept suggesting to everyone that a bear must have carried off Mrs. Inglis. After all, there are lots of them on this mountain. We may as well just give up searching for her if a bear carried her off, I kept suggesting. No one listened to me. Everyone just kept up their searching.

After the first day, some people had to go home to tend to animals and children, but others kept on searching. They made it all the way to Lequille, heard that she had her grain milled, and then the searchers headed back up the road again.

Mrs. Todd told the searchers how Mrs. Inglis had stopped in for a cup of tea and ate her bread and cheese while resting her feet, and had gone on her way again. It was the last person they could find who saw her.

The search party was getting tired by now and decided to stop and take a break at the Perotte brook. One of the searchers, Maggie Durling, needed to relieve herself. Leaving the group for some privacy, Maggie made for an old overturned tree for some privacy.

It was said that you could hear her screams all the way to the Buckler Inn.

Everyone looked at me.

~

It didn't take long for the township people to figure out that it was John Gregory who had done this to me. He wasn't at his shop on the day I left for the grist mill in Lequille. Colonel Ramsay told how he found John Gregory in his barn that night. Everyone recalled him blathering on and on about a bear carrying me off.

After my body was brought back to the township and I was buried, Samuel turned on his heel and walked all the way to Annapolis Royal to talk with the sheriff. The sheriff and two constables returned on horseback with Samuel and they arrested John Gregory right then.

John Gregory spent the next two months in the gaol before his trial for murdering me. It didn't take long for the Grand Jury to find him guilty and sentence him to hang two weeks later.

I was there for the hanging. Before I moved on to my reward, I wanted to make certain that John Gregory paid the ultimate price for what he did to me. So I stayed around, watched things from a distance.

I watched Samuel grieve and rage; I watched my children cry over me as they buried my broken body. And I waited. I waited for John Gregory to be found guilty and punished.

I quietly watched him, crying as he walked to the noose hanging from the sturdy branch of an old willow tree in front of the court-house in Annapolis Royal. The Old Hanging Tree, they called it. People came from far and wide to watch the hanging of John Gregory.

John Gregory cried as they put the black hood on his head, he said he was so sorry for what he did to me, that he didn't mean to do it but he just wanted me to love him and I wouldn't. So he killed me in a fit of rage. He didn't mean to do it, he cried over and over again.

And then, just like he could see through that black hood, he looked right at me. He could see me where no one else here could. His eyes were filled with joy and tears and he said to me, "I'm coming to join you, Mother."

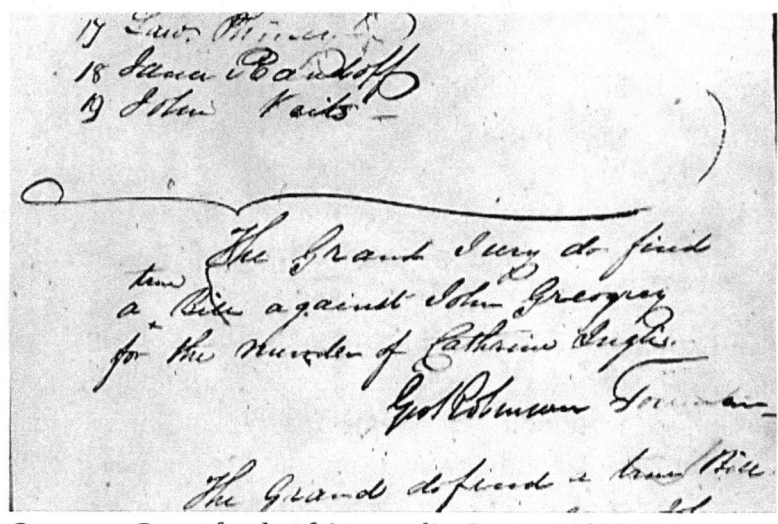

Supreme Court fonds of Annapolis County, 1833 Nova Scotia Archives: "The Grand Jury do find a true Bill against John Gregory for the murder of Catherine Inglis – Geo. Robinson, Foreman"

Acadian Recorder Newspaper September 21, 1833: "The Supreme Court closed its sittings at Annapolis on Friday week, when John Gregory, convicted of the murder of Catherine Inglis, was sentenced to die."

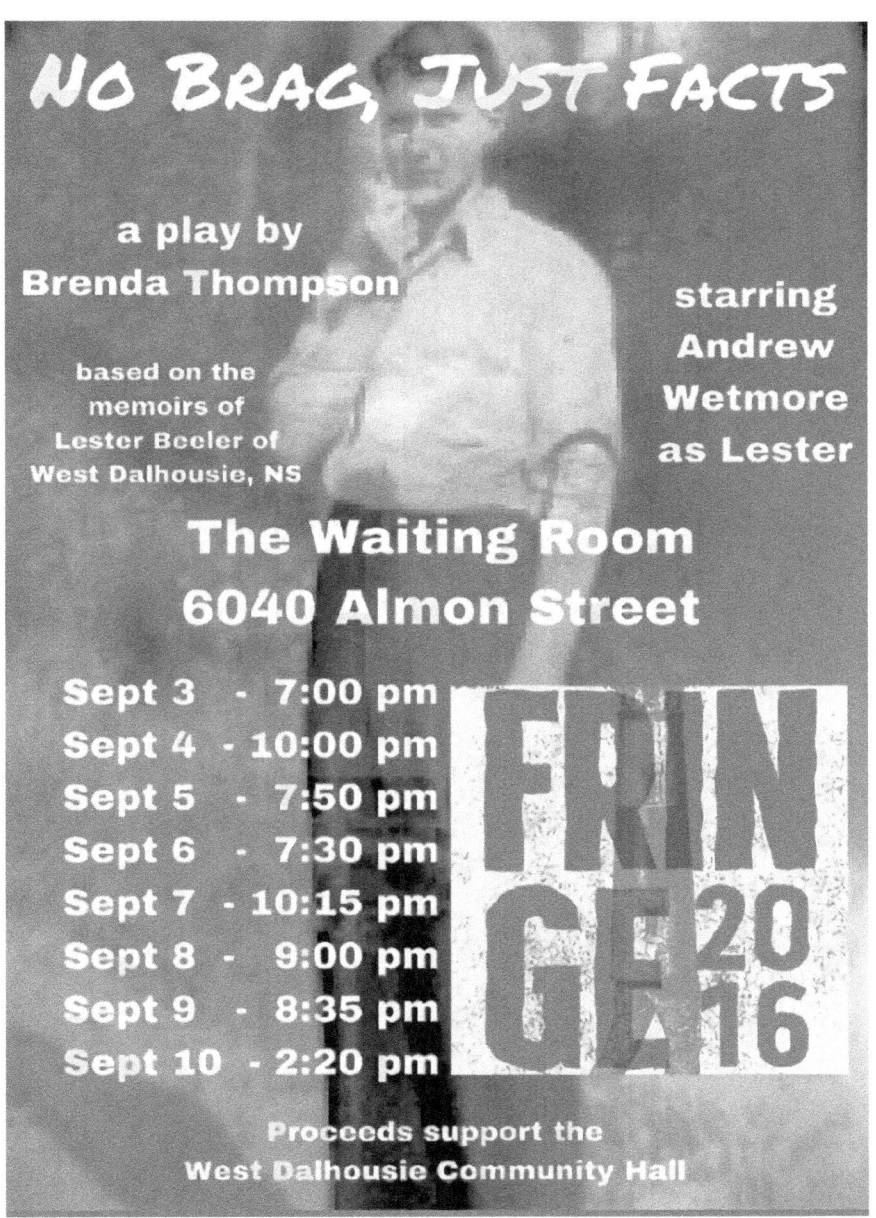

No Brag, Just Facts

Based on the memories of Lester Beeler

Lester Beeler lived in West Dalhousie for many years and, with his wife, raised four daughters. This piece is based on the play that I was commissioned to write for the West Dalhousie Community Hall. Andrew Wetmore performed the part of Lester Beeler in this one-person show. The play was hugely successful and went on to be performed by Andrew at the Fundy Fringe Festival in Saint John, New Brunswick, the Atlantic Fringe Festival in Halifax, Nova Scotia, and in community halls throughout the Annapolis Valley.

    This compilation is based on Lester's Memories with permission of Sharon Cranton, Lester's eldest daughter. Thank you, Sharon!

The story of my life

My soul! Look at all you people here tonight just to hear about me and my life in the settlement of West Dalhousie!

Now, before I get telling you my story, I want to let you know that what I am talking about is all facts; No brag, just facts.

Well, I guess, I had better just get on with it.

I am writing this memoir in the year 1990. The story of my life, which started somewhere in England in the year 1918 and on February 20th to be exact. That was the day of my birth, at night.

Mother always told me that it was during the First World War and that there was an air raid on that night that I was born.

My mother was an English woman and her father was an Englishman, but her mother came from Wales.

My father was Canadian-born, from the Annapolis Royal area. He came from a large family of ten. My people on my father's side came from Germany and their name was spelled "Büler", but George Büler, who came to Canada around 1700, changed his name to Beeler and we still use that name to this day.

In my own family I had two brothers and two sisters and I was the first born.

My mother and I came from to Nova Scotia from England on a boat. We landed in New York City and then went on another boat to Annapolis Royal in 1918.

We lived in a small house in Annapolis Royal, close to a pond of water which was, at that time, a small hydro system that made electric power for the town. It seems that mother had let me outdoors and somehow I toddled over and fell into the pond. After a while, mother came looking for me and there I was, floating around in the pond. So she swam out and pulled me to shore and saved me.

In Bridgetown

I remember the year 1921 when we lived in Bridgetown. It was here that mother used to tie me with a rope outside on the lawn and this worked fine, I guess, until the day I got loose. Leaving all clothes behind, I proceeded to go to town in my birthday suit. Some kind lady, I don't recall her name, brought me back home again.

About this time, the ice took out the road bridge in Bridgetown and people had to get across the river by boat. You could also walk across the railway bridge, which I do remember a bit about. Dad carried my sister Joan in one arm and led me by the hand so I could step from one tie to the other. I can remember looking down and seeing the water and ice going under the bridge.

The tide used to come up the river in those days, but since the installation of the causeway, the tide does not come up anymore now. I remember a story about a man who owned a sailing vessel coming up the river with the tide. They were headed for the bridge so he told his helper to throw over the anchor. The man said there was no rope on it. The Captain said, "Throw it, anyway and it might stop our headway some!"....and I guess the anchor is still at the bottom of the river to this day!

West Dalhousie

Eventually we moved to the settlement of West Dalhousie, up on top of the South Mountain, seven miles outside of Bridgetown.

There are so many things for me to write about in my 72 years. I can remember my dad wanting to get his 1923 Overland car greased, so my sister and I got a can of Vagon grease and did the job for him. Only, we greased the seats, the steering wheel, the tires and everything but the right thing. Anyway, we did not sit down for about a week after that.

I can remember going to the little old school house and the hard old teacher we had. We had to toe the line, and if we did not learn, we got education pounded in with the oak stick.

We had to walk to school those days in all kinds of weather, and times were hard. I saw one bunch of kids from one family come to school in their bare feet. We ate bread and molasses along with some spring water which we drank while kneeling down to get it. Sometimes we had a birch bark cup.

I remember, at about age 7 or 8, I had to milk and tend a cow and a pig and keep the wood box full of wood.

Old Joe

I remember a story that happened when I was 5 or 6 years old.

Old Joe was a Jew from Syria. He came to Nova Scotia as a young man and learned English. At first he walked the roads selling pencils, spools of thread and most anything that could be carried in a pack sack.

As time went on, he got more well to do and had a house which he used as a store and a place to live. He had a horse to haul his wagon and the horse's name was Pilot.

After a while, he got a Model T Ford truck which he learned to drive, but not too well.

Millie, the school teacher, was teaching school a few miles from her home so she had to board in the area. On Friday nights, she would come home for the weekend, and it happened that Joe was in the area one Friday night in the autumn. So Millie hitched a ride home with Joe. He had his old truck which was loaded with groceries and feed which he was peddling out.

Well, Old Joe and Millie were starting for home, but somehow Joe lost control and the truck landed in a lake and the water came right up into the cab. There was Millie sitting in the water.

Joe got out and got to shore. This was in the fall, mind you, and the ground was frozen and ice was in the water so it must have been cold.

Joe left Millie in the truck and walked to the nearest house, crying, "I am dying!"

The people in the house said, "You old fool, you are just wet and you are not likely to die."

Anyway, the folks there helped to get Millie out of the truck and with oxen they pulled the old truck out of the water. Millie and Joe had to walk home after they dried out.

It has been told that the people there went to the lake with hooks and fished out bars of soap and tobacco for days after.

Now remember, folks, this is no brag; just facts!

Hard times

Times were hard in my early years. I can remember waking up one morning in the 20s and my father was boring a hole in a five gallon keg of bootleg rum. It was so strong it would burn like gasoline. These were in the rum running days and someone in Annapolis Royal used to pick it up on the South Shore and sell it to anyone who would buy it.

The price then was $25.00 for five gallons. They would make ten gallons out of five gallons by using half water, and even then you could not drink it without adding more water.

Mother was a great one to raise flowers in her garden and did a lot of digging and hoeing. Every once in a while she would dig up a bottle of rum dad had buried in the garden.

Later in the 20s, we had the first radio come to our home. In those days we used earphones to listen and we had two sets of those.

One night there was a boxing match on in America somewhere. It was between Jack Dempsey and Jack Sharky. We could just barely hear the action and dad had invited in quite a few neighbours to hear the fight of fifteen rounds. So whoever had the earphones on would tell the others how the fight was going; even blow by blow was told. Also, they had some homemade beer which helped to make things more interesting.

After a time, later on, we got a very large speaker, or horn as us kids called it. Then we could all hear what there was to hear. All the radio signals in those days came from America. There was none in Canada, least not in our area.

After a year or so, Dad and I put in a water wheel at a pond of water that was by the old stave mill. This gave us some electric power to run the radio and some lights. The voltage was 32 volts

DC. We had the first lights in our area.

This involved a job for me on the way to school. I would stop the wheel during the day then on my way home at night I would start the wheel up again after I serviced the machine. This involved oil and grease and a check of the belts, etc.

There were no fridges those days so if you wanted to keep milk and butter it was either down cellar or hanging them in the well.

One hard winter

One winter our father had to go to the hospital in Halifax to have an operation. The year was 1930 and times were very hard. There was no work and no money and not much to eat. It was during the Depression and everyone was hard put to make a living.

As Dad was a veteran from the war of 1918, and had a bad case of the piles, he decided to go to the Veterans' Hospital in Halifax and have the piles operated on.

So off he went, and left us kids and his wife home in the old log house with no money and no wood to keep up warm.

I was 12 years old at the time, so being the eldest, I decided that I should get to work. I could have went to school but we had to eat, so it is not much good to go to school if the grub is shy. There was no food and the store keepers would not let out anything without the money.

So mother and I set plans to do something about our lack of money and food and wood and, I give mother credit, she was the backbone and helped a lot.

At the time, we had a big male police dog named Pal. So I made a set of bobsleds with a rack on them and he and I set out to get the wood for the house. I sawed it with the old buck saw and split it with the axe. When I got a load, the dog and I would haul it to the house and we kept the family warm all winter.

Along with getting the wood, I had set about 300 rabbit snares in hedges and, as the rabbits were thick that winter, I did very well at snaring them. Every other Saturday, the dog and I would take a load of rabbits to town—a round trip of 14 miles—and I would sell them for fox feed for seven and a half cents a pair. Then I would bring grub home.

In the spring, I had two cords of wood piled when dad came home in April. He was gone all winter. You see, if he stayed in the hospital, he got some pension which he would not get at home. So he sent mother $7 a month to help out.

A near miss

Our home was a log cabin which my father had built. This building was built with round logs and a tar paper roof. Every fall we had to gather moss from the woods and stog up the openings between the logs.

I have laid in bed and from there I could see the stars shining through the cracks in the joint between the logs. We were a healthy, happy family in that cabin.

One day, when I was 12, I nearly shot my mother. You see, father had dug out a place for a cellar, only about four feet deep, so that when you were in the cellar, your head and shoulders were show-ing above the floor.

One day, I had my dad's 12 gauge pump shotgun and the gun held five shells in the magazine. I should have unloaded it outdoors but I had not done this, so I decided to do it in the house.

At 12 years old, I suppose I had no business with a gun of any kind and if my dad had known about it, I would have been picking splinters out of my ass.

Now this gun, you could pump the action and the shells would all come out. This was what I was doing and I thought the gun was empty, but it turned out it wasn't. So when I pulled the trigger, I thought I was doing so on an empty gun.

But this was not the case and, as I pulled the trigger, my mom's head popped up from the cellar and—BOOM!—the gun blew a hole in the floor about two feet from my mom.

I guess it wasn't her time to go and I wouldn't have wanted to live if I had shot my mother that day.

So after mum and I got over our scare, and believe me I was scared to death and so was Mother, we had to plug up the hole in the floor so my dad wouldn't see it. So I got a piece of wood and, with my knife, I made a plug to fit the hole. As we had no paint, I used shoe polish to stain the wood and mum put a mat over the place.

Dad wondered about the mat but he never did look under it. I guess if he had looked under it, my goose would have been cooked on that day for sure. Dad was a good man but he was rough on his family and we had to mind, one way or the other.

Into the Valley

Mother did not like where we were living, being born to the city life. She always wanted to get back to it. So Dad decided to move out of West Dalhousie to the Valley, where he bought a farm. A nice old place it was, too.

He had to borrow money to buy the place, which he did, thinking that he could raise and sell foxes to pay the mortgage.

So he built a new fox ranch right in the apple orchard and he had about 30 fox pups as I recall, plus quite a few old foxes.

Dad was sitting pretty, as the saying goes, only he had the apple trees sprayed and some of those trees were right in the fox pens. When the apples fell off the tees and into the pens, the foxes ate them and the poison killed every blessed fox. He lost every one of them.

So, in short, there went his deposit and the farm. We had to move back to the old place in the woods in West Dalhousie and he found himself around $5,000 in debt, and that was a lot of money in those days.

Deep in debt

At the time I was 13 and in Grade 8. Now the pinch came.

Dad said to me, "You will have to quit school and go to work with me in the old mill"...and me not old enough to smoke yet!!

I remember my first pay cheque; it was for $4.50 for the week and that was for 59 hours of work.

I worked at the stave mill, making material for apple barrels. And for the next 4 or 5 years, I helped him pay off the debt and I never did see a pay cheque beyond that first one.

I got my clothes and enough to eat and did some fishing and hunting and going to church and house parties. This applied to all the young people in our area, but they were good times. We had not much money but we had good health and that meant a lot.

It was an election year in the fall of 1936 and I was 18 years old. I did not have a vote but I drove my dad's car and took people to the polls. Those days you could buy votes for $5. In those days $5 was a lot of money....a week's pay for a lot of people. As I mentioned, I was working 59 hours a week for $4.50.

A one-man band

Along about this time I got my first guitar and started picking on that. As time went on I got a drum, and I could play the mouth organ. After a while I started playing in the dance halls. I had a one man band. I beat the drum with my foot and I had a rack that held the mouth organ.

Most times the dance would start about 9 pm and run until 12:30 or 1 am. I did this two or three times a week for quite a few years.

My first fiddle was a copy of a Stradivarius and is an old one I bought it for $10 from a coloured lady years ago. Her father brought it up the river on a sailing ship around the turn of the century. Her father, who brought the fiddle, lived to be 100 years old and came up from the southern states. It is said they he could remember the slave days.

Anyway, I brought that fiddle out at Christmas times, and a lot of fiddle players have tried to buy it from me, but I am planning on leaving it to my second girl when I pass away.

I have always loved to play music and still do so in my retirement.

Anyway, that was just a few of the things I did to earn money. I worked for other people in these mills at different times and learned the business from the ground up until I could do any job there was to do, even getting to do the sawing.

Our family was all girls

Along about 1938, I believe, I had a girlfriend. She was an old schoolmate, if you like. Anyway, after a time we decided to get married. I had bought her an engagement ring from the catalogue for $15 on the instalment plan. I think it was $1 a month.

So on April 15th, on a Saturday night, we got married and moved into our rented cabin, which cost us $5 a month. We only rented it for one month then we bought it for $75 and paid for it at $5 a month. It was nice and it was our first home.

After about three years and a lot of work and concentration, my wife came out with our first daughter, and what a bouncer she was!

I remember when she was about three months old and I was coming home one week in December, I think. I had to work away that winter to make a living so I only got home on Saturday night and had to go back on Sunday night.

Anyway, it seems the baby had been fussy all week and my wife resorted to rocking her, which was habit-forming. No sooner had I got in the house when she informed me that I would have to rock the child to give her a rest.

So, me not being experienced in this field, I did it for about four hours and finally the baby went to sleep.

Well sir, during the next week at work I decided that the business of rocking a baby wasn't for me. So I had to figure out a way to solve the problem.

When I came home the next weekend, of course I was presented with the same problem. So I asked, "Is the baby sick?"

The answer was, "No, she is just fussy and wants to cry if she is not rocked."

I said, "No, I am not rocking her. Put her in the crib."

Well sir, of all the crying you ever heard, she done. But after about two hours of crying and sobbing, she went to sleep. The rocking chair did not get worn out and lasted for years. And there were three more baby girls to come into our house after that.

Our family was all girls. The doctor could not seem to put a handle on any of them.

My two oldest daughters were born during the Second World War. I wasn't able to go to war. I did try to join up in '39 but was turned down because of a hernia.

So I stayed home, got a family started and did what I could on the home front to keep the population up.

Since the old doctor could not get me any boys, I had to work the girls like boys. Jobs like putting in the wood for winter and snow shovelling and all jobs that boys should be doing and they did not like.

Our second little girl came along about two years after the first one. She was born in October and she now tells me that for quite a few years, she thought she was a boy.

Wheels

Now, I liked my cars and trucks back then. I still do, but I liked to buy a car or truck on a deal and then fix it up. Over a period of about 52 years, my cost for cars was only about $11,000 which is a record I believe.

But I also used a bicycle to get around in those days. One time I remember coming home after dark, riding my bike, and in those days we had no light, but we could see well enough in the dark.

Anyway, my brother-in-law and I popped over a little hill and I put the front wheel of my bike right between the hind legs of a cow moose that was standing in the road. I did not get hurt and the moose was none the worse, but it gave me quite a scare.

Remember, no brag, just facts.

A crash

One morning in April, 1941, I believe, during the Second World War, someone at the Greenwood Air Base at Kingston called me to the phone at around 2 am. They told me that they just had a Mosquito bomber go down at Mud Lake, which was around 10 miles from where I lived. They wanted me to go and see if I could help if someone was hurt.

By the time I got ready to go, the phone was ringing again. It was the base again and they had changed their minds. The plane was down in Lohnes Lake, which was a different kettle of fish.

Since it was four miles, we decided to wait until daylight to start looking. Like I said, it was April and there was lots of snow and water around and the roads were mud to the axle. In those days there was no pavement in our area.

Anyway, the base sent down a truck load of grub and about 50 English airmen who were with an ox team to haul the food and equipment into the area where the plane crashed.

The airmen that were brought into the village to help search kept taking off in the woods, getting lost, and we would have to go hunt them up and bring them out. So we decided to get the head man of their group to send them home as we could see they were going to be no good to us, which is what he did.

Then, with a Canadian flying officer, we started to look for the plane. I had never been to Lohnes Lake before so it was new country to me. The officer with me said if we get close to the plane, we would likely smell glycol, which is what they used in all the radiators.

Anyway, we travelled around the lake quite close to the shore. We went all the way around and did not see any sign of a plane, but when we crossed the outlet of the lake, I thought I could smell something.

The officer couldn't smell it so we decided to go around again. This time I made a wider circle and stayed farther from the lake shore.

We were following along a game trail through the snow and wet bushes and by this time we were really wet and discouraged. I might add that I was travelling ahead.

As I passed by a bush, I looked down to the ground and saw something there. I could not make out what it was so I bent down and picked it up.

It was a man's head....flattened out like a pancake, and the hair was brown and very curly.

So we marked the area on the trees with blazes and at about this time there was a plane flying low up above us so we knew we must be close to the crash.

We kept going in the direction we thought was right. The farther west, the more plane parts and parts of human bodies we found until we came to the place where the plane had hit the ground. It was right at the edge of a swamp.

That was a Wednesday and we could not do any more then. The officer took charge and said we could not touch anything. He would have to bring in investigators from Ottawa. So we all went home.

By Saturday, the base called again, saying they were coming on Sunday to go to the site of the crash and wanted us to go with them. A few of us went along with them, not knowing what was going to be done.

Once we got there, there was a Padre and they were carrying some large burlap bags. When we saw these we began to figure things out.

At the crash site we were asked to help find as much of the two airmen as possible. Which we did.

It was quite a job but we did good, I think, as none of us had ever seen anything like this. We collected a lot of pieces and used hand borrows made from plane parts to carry the men to their last resting place.

You see, these men came from England to train here and at that time there was no way they would get back to their native homeland. The Padre gave us a choice and it was up to us to decide whether we would carry them out in the bags on our backs, or let them be buried at the site.

We decided that they should stay with their plane so we buried them there and had a funeral service for them. And the men are still buried there to this day. The rings and watches of the men were sent to their relatives and, I believe, some of their relatives have been over to visit their graves.

Our people of the settlement frowned on us for deciding to bury the men with their plane crash but we thought we had done the right thing. To this day, I think we did the right thing,

The box of red paper

My soul, we need a happier story after that one. So I will tell you about the box of red paper.

One Christmas morning, my wife and I were getting things ready for our girls as my wife was very fussy with things like that. It was about 2 am and it was a cold night with snow on the ground.

We had just decided to go to bed when there came a knock on our door. I went to the door, wondering who in the hell that could be. I knew Santa always stopped at our place first, but he never knocked on the door.

Anyway, when I opened the door, there stood a neighbour of ours, a woman, no less, and she lived a half mile from our place. She was some cold and shook like a leaf.

Well, we let her in where it was warm and got her a cup of tea. After a while, she got around to tell me her troubles.

She said her husband had come home drunk and had forgot to pick up some Christmas presents for their grandchildren. She wanted to know if I would go and get the presents at a friend's house out towards town, about five miles away.

So I thought, being Christmas and all, I would do it for her. So off we went in my old Erskine car.

We arrived at the place where the presents were supposed to be and she went in the house and I stayed in the car. I could watch through the window, and I saw them pass her a box with some red paper sticking out of it. So I felt better.

Now all I had to do was get her back home, but this was not to be.

When she got back in the car, she said, "Would you take me down to the bootlegger? I want to get some rum."

I again thought, it being Christmas and all, how could I refuse her?

Off we went to the bootlegger to get the rum and me wondering what my wife was thinking. I knew she would wait up for me.

So after pounding on the bootlegger's door at 3 a.m. for about half an hour, he finally got up and opened his door. I see right off that she knew him and had done business there before.

She soon came to the car with her rum and then we started for home.

She even knew where all the little brooks were along the road. The first one we came to, she said, "Stop here and we will have a drink"

So, like I said, it being Christmas time and all, how could I refuse her?

Anyway, after the drinks, I went on home to her place and she invited me in.

And, it being Christmas time and all....

But I declined and said, "No, thanks. I better get home as Santa would likely be there and I always have tea with him."

Off I went home and put the car in the garage and went into the house. My wife was still up and I had to swear on the bible that I had not tested that woman's wares.

Now, would you believe it? I got into bed and was nearly asleep when it came to me. I said, "My God! That woman forgot her Christmas presents. They are still in the car."

So, being Christmas time and all, I said, "I will have to take them back to her."

I got up and dressed up again and went to the car. I started it up and backed it out and started on the road to her place.

All at once I thought, "That's funny that she would forget that box."

I stopped to have a look in the box and, you know, all that was in the box was red paper, some ribbon off parcels and a few name tags. Now, you see, this was a story she had made up to get me to go and get the rum. She knew if she had told me that all she wanted was the rum, I would not likely have gone to get it for her.

Anyway, I got taken on that deal and the good Lord was on my side, like he always is. This woman was hard on the men like some women are, but she was a good woman in other ways.

So here ends another true story.

A fishing story

It's time for a fishing story! My soul, I did a lot of fishing and hunting when we lived in the settlement. I fed my family nothing but fish and moose and deer. Now my daughters won't touch the stuff. All they will eat is pork and beef. They must have had too much of the wild stuff growing up.

Anyway, I always planned a fishing trip in May and took four or five days off from work. Well, this trip turned out to be a dandy, as I will tell you.

There were no roads in the back of the county in those days, and you walked and travelled by boat or canoe. Myself and three other friends set out in the morning after being dropped off at Curl Hole flowage in back of New Albany.

After crossing two or three small lakes and carrying our gear over three canoe carries, we arrived at Alma Lake around 10 pm. It was dark and foggy on the lake and a bit of rain was coming down.

There was an old lumber camp on this lake that we wanted to get to, but after going around and around on the lake in the fog, we seemed lost and could not find the place where the camp was.

Being wet and cold, my friend in my canoe broke out a bottle of rum and we had some to drive away the cold. Now, you should all know that rum and canoes don't mix.

So I said, "We are lost. We can't find the camp in the dark so if we can hit shore, that's where we better stay the night."

After a while we landed on a beach and pulled our canoes ashore. We had no light but I managed to cut a dead, dry pine tree so we got a fire going and things looked better.

We boiled up some tea and heated up a large pan of baked beans and right there started getting into the hooch.

We had drank the rum so someone broke out a bottle of whisky and soon it went down to mix up with the beans. Then someone produced some old sour cider in Milk of Magnesia bottles. The tea was all gone by then so we drank the cider to wash down the bread and beans.

Well you can see we had done a bad thing to our digestive systems and they were not willing to accept all this without complaining.

As I said, we were all wet, tired, sleepy and quite drunk. In those days, no one had sleeping bags; we just laid down on the ground and slept like an animal.

Anyway, we had laid down and were off to slumberland when sometime in the night my friend said, "My God! There's a bear here with us!".

Sure enough, there was a bear looking us over. Us, being drunk, didn't give a damn for the bear and rolled over and went back to sleep. The bear, not liking the odour we were giving off anyway, ambled off to where the air was cleaner.

However, when it became daylight, we had sobered up and I felt none too bad.

My friend, however, was some sick. He kept saying, "I think I am gonna die," and he looked bad. He was white as a ghost and had heaved up some of the booze and beans.

He wanted to go back home but we said that if he just would hang in for while, he will be okay. So I proceeded to load up the canoe to get ready to find the camp. I was using a small canoe, only an 11 foot one, but it was a good one, nonetheless.

As soon as I was ready to depart, I went to find my friend but he was so sick that he could not help me. When I found him, he felt so bad that he was on his knees praying to the Lord saying, "Lord, I am too young to die yet. Can't you just give me one more chance and I promise not to get drunk anymore and I won't bother any more married women."

I got him in the canoe and he laid right down in the bottom of it and groaned and slept most of the day. I paddled along and caught some trout. I would take them off the hook and throw them right on top of him. I could see that he was breathing so I knew he was not dead even then he didn't complain about me throwing fish on him.

Eventually we found the camp and I put my friend in the bed and covered him up. I gave him a full glass of gin as that was all I had for medicine. My friend soon dropped off to sleep and slept right through till morning.

The next morning he seemed completely healed and I got us some breakfast. My friend ate so much food for his breakfast that we were short of food for the rest of the trip.

We caught a lot of trout and we ate some of them. But you know, my friend never drank old cider mixed with whisky since then.

And my advice to you, folks, is to never drink old cider and whisky and eat homemade baked beans because they don't seem to mix well.

We got home safe and sound and started thinking about our next trip. My friend is still living at 82 years old and still smokes and chews tobacco. He takes a little drink once in a while but I don't know if he kept his vow to God about the married women.

But all is well that ends well.

There is so many stories I could tell you, but we haven't got all night, so I have to just pick out the good ones.

Two green eyes

Now this story is about a hunting and trapping trip to Long Lake in the late 20s. The country back then was pretty wild so no one got in there too often. It was all walking and canoe work. There were a few old hunting camps but no roads.

In those days the moose were thick and it was no trouble to get one any time, but we were like the Mi'kmaq and only killed when we needed the meat.

On this trip, Dad had gone trapping for muskrat, mink, fox, otter weasel and squirrel. In the evening, Dad and Stanley were jacking for deer and using a two-cell flashlight. They were upstairs in an old horse barn. The owners had moved away.

Anyway, around 11 pm, when they turned on their light, they saw two green eyes. So dad lined up his old 8mm rifle and let go. The eyes went out of sight, so they thought they had got whatever it was.

They rushed to the area as fast as they could with the aid of the light. They came across a very large buck deer and he looked quite dead.

Dad laid down his gun and took hold of the deer horns. "Good Lord, Stan," he said. "What a monster!"

Right about then, the deer came to his feet and took off, with Dad hanging on the horns. Seems like Dad's shot had only stunned the deer and it was none the worse for wear.

Dad was dropped to the ground and said that if he ever had the chance again, he'd make sure that deer was dead before he picked up his horns.

Oh my.

Swimming

There are a lot of lakes and swimming holes around West Dalhousie and my mom taught all us kids how to swim when we were kids. She was a good swimmer and I have swam long distances with her.

In the summer we swam just about every swimming hole we came across. Most of the time we swam naked because we were too poor to own swimsuits.

However, on the occasion when Fred nearly drowned, I was married then and lived with my wife by the lake. It was a Sunday and it was hot and a lot of people were cooling off in the lake....all but me. I was sitting on the veranda having a cigarette. I smoked in those days. That was before I knew any better.

Anyway, Fred and his two brothers were out to a raft we used for diving. It was off quite a ways, and they had been swimming and diving out there for some time. People on shore were not paying any attention to the people on the raft, including me. We had some company and were seeing who could tell the biggest lie about some fish we had caught.

All at once, everyone got excited and shouted, "Someone is in trouble in the water."

They were calling for help, so I ran down to see if I could help and soon I saw it was Fred. He took to cramps and could not move and his brothers were trying to help him, but were tired out themselves.

So off with my pants and in I went to try and help him.

I will never forget that day and he won't either, I don't think. When I got close to him, he was a calm as anything and he said, "My God, I can't do a thing!"

I said, "No matter, Fred. Just hang on and I will get you to shore."

I towed him to shore and you know he never lets me forget that day. He lives today with his wife not too far away and I see him once in a while.

Another fellow got into trouble there one day. He could not swim and here again, I had to shed my pants. Only this time I had no undies on.

When I got close to the fellow, I was a bit scared myself. He was really terrified and was grabbing at me and he had an awful look on his face.

I thought, "Boy, you're not going to get a hold of me. I want to live a bit longer."

I balled a fist and hit him right between the eyes and he seemed to go to sleep. Then I had no trouble to get him to shore.

So after I got him to shallow water, someone else dragged him to shore and my wife brought me a pair of shorts. She said she didn't want the other ladies there to see the size of my bird or they would be after me all the time. So I put the shorts on underwater and the ladies never did see anything!!

Anyway, soon after he was ashore, he started to cough and after a while he seemed okay. He may still be living today somewhere.

You see, I never did know who he was, and he nor anyone ever said Thanks, but I felt good about it just the same.

Anyhow, I am so thankful that my mother had taught me to swim and that I had no fear of the water.

Joe and Tid

Now, let me tell you about some of my friends and neighbours.

Let me tell you about Joe and Tid. They were brothers and they have now done on to the happy hunting grounds. I knew them both and they would be tickled to know that I am telling you this story about them.

Joe was a great fella and some good hunter and a great shot. Old Tid was a blacksmith, and a good one in his day. Those were the days when you worked for 50 cent a day or $12 a month and you had to board yourself and sleep on a straw tick in the bed.

In those days some of the men used to go to Maine to work in the woods there. This time Joe and Tid had gone to Bangor to work in the woods. I don't know how they got there, but somehow they did.

They were both big men and not afraid of anything or anyone. They had no education and had never gone to school because they had to go to work or starve.

They got to Bangor and went into a hotel there to spend the night. The next day they planned to get into the woods to work in a lumber camp. At the hotel desk they inquired about a room and the clerk told them there was no rooms left and he could not take them in.

Now, you see, the weather was cold and it was raining and just a terrible night. So they asked, "Well, we could stay most anywhere. Surely you must have something."

"Well," the clerk said, "of course there is the attic, but there is nothing but an old mattress up there. But there is a problem with the flies up there. They are awful thick. If you don't mind the flies, you would be welcome to the attic."

"Okay, we'll take it," they said. "We don't have a choice, I guess."

The next morning the manager had breakfast with the boys and found out that they came from Nova Scotia. He was curious and wanted to know how they made out with all the flies in the attic.

Joe and Tid said, "Oh, that was no problem. We just bunched them up."

The manager asked, "What do you mean?"

The boys replied, "Well we just shit in one corner of the attic and that kept the flies all in one place."

The manager, you see, thought these were just a couple of dumb Nova Scotian boys who never went to school. Joe and Tid showed him!

A wood frolic

This time I am going to tell you about what happened at Old Abe's. Old Abe was ailing and needed help, so the neighbours put on a wood frolic to saw and split some wood for him.

The day was set up and a lot of men showed up to do the job.

Now, in those days, most every household had a keg of home brew and, sure enough, Abe had on a barrel of the stuff and it was well worked out and strong like rum. But Abe made the mistake of getting the beer out before the wood was cut and soon everyone was feeling good and the wood cutting was out of the question.

Then the fun started. I remember one fellow went into the hen coop and grabbed a big old rooster by the legs. He brought it outdoors and with a big effort he threw the rooster way up in the air. The rooster flew right over the barn and they say Abe never saw the rooster again.

Like I said, as the barrel got drank up, the drunker everyone got.

Also, in those days, they would put on big feeds for dinner and supper. All the women would cook for the wood frolic. There would be baked beans and casseroles of all kinds and lot of pickles, brown bread, cakes and cookies.

In those days, everyone kept cows and had their own milk and butter. Oh, yes, we could be having homemade jam or jelly or molasses. As you can see, the food was plain and we had to make do with whatever we had and I must say, we lived good in those days.

Anyway, on that day at old Abe's at dinner time, everyone was up high on Abe's beer and there was a round pad of homemade butter on the table. Old Hall, with his old bald head, was dishing up some stew on his plate when Howard, sitting next to him, thought it would be a good idea to grease old Hall's bald head with the butter.

So he did. And after putting it back on the plate, everyone proceeded to apply the butter to their bread and did not seem to mind the taste at all.

The wood never did get sawed and split on that day.

Ralph

Now, I cannot tell you about my life without telling you about Ralph.

Poor old Ralph is dead and gone these last ten years but he is not forgotten. A good man and a good friend. He was a hard man on the rum bottle and did not like to eat anything that was sweet. He smoked three packs of cigarettes a day for as long as I can remember.

We had a lot of trips together and he was a lot of fun, but my, how he could snore. He could make the stove covers jump up and down with his snoring. When Ralph and I would go on a hunting or fishing trip overnight, I would always try to fall asleep first cause there was no sleeping when Ralph fell asleep and started snoring.

Ralph always liked me to cook him what he called An Egg in a Hole. That was an egg fried in the centre of a piece of toast.

Ralph has scared me on a couple of occasions as well. One time we were gonna head out to go hunting and Ralph wanted to take his truck.

I said, "Ralph, you better fix that front tire. I can see the tube sticking out through a hole in the tire."

"Oh," he said, "That's okay. It's been that way all summer. It should be all right."

So I said, "All right." but I didn't feel good about it.

Off we went to his camp and he drove like the mill tails of hell. He went so fast that I did not need to take anything to loosen my bowels for a whole week after that.

He said, as we went along, "What's that awful smell here in the car?"

I said, "That's the fruits of your dangerous driving, but as soon as I can change my shorts, I think the smell will go away."

After our hunting trip, we made it back to Ralph's truck and found that the tire with the tube sticking out of it had gone flat. I said we should put the spare on the truck and Ralph agreed, but when we went to get the spare tire, we found it was flat as well.

Well, Ralph said we should just change the tires anyway so we took off the flat and put on a flat...which made no sense but we did it.

Now, as it happened, we were at the foot of quite a high hill and it was all rocks and they were sharp. So Ralph poured on the coal, as he used to say, and the stones flew out from under the hind wheels. I stood back out the way while he tore his way up the hill. He stopped at the top and when I got to him, I could hear the air going out of a hind tire.

Ralph said, "Jump in and we will go as far as we can. Keep watch of the hind tire."

He wanted me to let him know before it got right out of air. So I hung out the truck window and watched the tire. Soon I told him that the time had come and we stopped and took the tire off the wheel. Also, by this time, the tire on the front wheel had come off on its own so now we had two wheels running with no tires.

We went on and after a while, we got to a service station and we had some tires put on.

Sometimes Ralph was a nuisance, especially when he would get too much rum in his old belly. But then he had not much to live for. His wife was dead and he had no interest in the women. He did have a way with old cars and done all his own engine work.

Crib

Well, time is getting on. The wife must be wondering where I am by now.

It is January 10, 1993 as I write this. We're living in Bridgetown now, down the mountain from West Dalhousie.

So as I sit here in the house in Bridgetown, looking out across the street at the funeral parlour where I will probably end up someday soon, I am waiting for Alice to wake up so she can beat me at crib.

My health has been going downhill now for some time and I have been trying to stay alive, because I like life here and because I want to take care of my dear old wife as long as I can.

If I have to go first, I wish the Lord would let me take her with me. We have been so happy together all these years.

You see, I have been told that I have cancer of the blood and bone marrow, so I may not be here too long, it seems. I am taking some pills with the hope that they will help the problem.

However, I have always said that I would not linger and suffer like I have seen some poor souls. I may have to help things along somehow. Now, I know the Lord will frown on me but this is my belief even though I may have to pay for it in the hereafter.

As I see it, I have quite a few things wrong in my body to contend with. As long as I feel half well, I will carry on. But if and when I get worse, I will likely go fishing someday and forget to come back.

Anyway, on this day, I feel pretty well so I will wake Alice up to get her to play Crib with me. I hope my family will keep this book after I am gone.

And maybe I will get to cook old Ralph the egg in the hole again sometime.

Brenda J. Thompson

Ernest in the Settlement

Ernest Buckler made a major contribution to Canadian literature from his farm far from the Toronto scene. His achievements, includ- ing the celebrated novel The Mountain and the Valley, are all real, but the interaction between him and the character of Sarah is com- pletely fictional.

They sat in the forest bower and stuck their toes in the water. It was early April and the water was what his mother would call "re- freshing". Her mother would admonish her for not only taking her wool stockings off in front of a boy but also for endangering herself with an illness that she may catch from the cold water and air. After all, had her father not just died?

Sarah did not care. It wasn't just any boy, it was Ernest Buckler. He was sweet and caring and listened to her. He did not try to im- press her with how strong he was. He was not loud; he did not flex his muscles and whip his oxen in a show of physical strength. No, Ernest took lessons in Greek and Latin; he wrote poetry and stor- ies. His uncle Wallace was preparing him to enter University and leave this little settlement.

Ernest was smart; smarter than any other boy in the school. Which was why the other boys teased him and called him girlish names. Which was why most of the girls liked him, protected him, mothered him and loved him. He, in turn, read his stories and poetry to them. Some of the girls wanted to marry him when they grew up but their mothers said he would make a terrible farmer or woodsman and they would always be poor because you cannot live off poetry.

Ernest never claimed he was going to be a farmer or a woodsman. He had always been planning on leaving the settlement and getting his Baccalaureate degree. He wanted to travel around the world on the wings of his education.

His uncle Wallace had been a soldier in the Great War of 1914 and travelled to Europe. Uncle told stories of sidewalk cafés in Paris, where painters and poets sipping tiny little coffees that exploded with flavour, and shared their creations to make your mind whirl with pleasure. Of London, and theatre performances that made you weep. Of Italy, where the restaurants served food seductive with flavour.

What Uncle Wallace did not speak about were his schoolmates, his neighbours, who went to Europe with him and did not come back. He did not speak of the bloodied, mangled, unrecognizable bodies. He did not speak of living weeks at a time in trenches where he shared his rations with the rats. Nor did he speak of his greatest love, whom he left, had to leave behind.

Uncle Wallace just wanted Ernest to see that there was more to life than farming on thin, rocky soil or felling trees in the dark, cold forests of the mountain. "There is more to life," he told Ernest, "than marrying the girl down the road and having too many children whom you cannot feed or clothe properly, for whom you work your life's essence away to raise and protect and shelter, only to have them break your heart by dying suddenly of a childhood disease or by growing up to forget you when you are old and need them."

Uncle Wallace knew that Ernest was different, like him. He wanted Ernest to see the world, taste it and feel all that the world had to offer.

Ernest was enthralled by the stories. He felt, sometimes, that he could almost touch these experiences Uncle Wallace wove with his words. He could not wait to feel these stories himself. He just did not understand why his uncle did not stay with his love, or bring his love here.

They had just attended the funeral of Sarah's dad, John, who had drowned in a logging accident. John had been trying to break up a jam of hardwood logs on Dargie Lake, moving them with his peavey. Hardwoods did not float well and were difficult to man-euver, but John was an experienced "river pig" and felt confident he could break up this jam.

But then the logs heaved and opened up underneath him and swallowed him.

John was shocked at first that this had happened to him. He fought the water and the logs, swam underneath looking for a lighter log that he could move so he could force his way up to air. All of the hardwood stayed firmly jammed together, not letting him see the sky again.

John eventually stopped fighting for air and relaxed, allowing the light from the bottom of the lake move toward him. In it he saw his father, who had died twelve years earlier, reaching out his hand to him. John was so happy to see him. He took his father's hand.

The other log drivers quickly moved to help John, to get him out from under the logs, but they could not retrieve him until the logs were moved to the sluice. Only then could they pull his lifeless body out from underneath the logs to bring him home for his fu-neral.

John's body was laid out in his coffin, resting on two chairs in the front parlour that was only used for special occasions such as this. The neighbours came by, paid their respects to the body, the widow and the children. John was eventually moved to the church where they prayed over his body and then buried him in the churchyard.

Sarah's mother, Mary, was beside herself with panic; not so much with grief, as she had never really loved John. But he was the first man to ask her for her hand in marriage. She was beside herself with worry about how she was going to support herself and her six children without his income. Sure, there was a widow's allowance she could get, but that would not be enough to support her and her children on this cursed farm of rocks.

Sarah felt her mother's panic. She knew their future as a family was in jeopardy. As the oldest girl of the family, at twelve years of age, Sarah knew she would be expected to leave school and get a job. She would probably have to move to Bridgetown and work as domestic helper and send her wages back to her mother to keep her out of the county home. It would be the only job available to a young woman such as herself.

She tucked her toes under her to warm them back up after the cool water as she sat there with Ernest on the forest floor. Even though Sarah was sad, Ernest felt content and full of life, feeling wondrously connected to this girl, his friend. And it was at this moment that Ernest and Sarah made a pact that they both regretted.

Ernest, sitting beside Sarah as she cried quietly, not only about the death of her father but also at what her future now held, wanted to make her feel better. He took her hand in his and quietly said, "Someday we'll get married, Sarah, and you won't have to work for rich people any more."

Sarah lifted her tear-stained face up to Ernest. Her eyes looked happier. "Really Ernest? Gosh, I would keep such a good house for you. You will have a warm hearth and good meals waiting for you when you come home from the woods. And you'll have many sons to crawl into your lap and grow up to help you with working in the woods."

Ernest, upon hearing her words, immediately began to regret his prophecy. What had he done? He wanted to get an education; he wanted to see the world. He did not want to marry and stay in this settlement all his life. What would Uncle Wallace say when he heard that Ernest had just promised Sarah he would marry her?

The forest bower ceased to be a delight and became dark and menacing to Ernest. He immediately wanted out.

"We should just keep this to ourselves," he said. "It's too soon after your father's death to tell everyone that we want to get married."

"Yes," she agreed, smiling through her sniffles. "Yes, you are right. But you have made me so happy, Ernest Buckler!"

She hugged him. Sarah had visions of her life with Ernest dancing through her head already. Her life of domestic drudgery would not be forever. She would have her own kitchen someday, and share it with the gentlest and kindest of men.

Ernest and Sarah kept this secret to themselves after that day. Ernest hoped Sarah would forget about it.

Sarah did indeed move off the mountain and into Bridgetown, where she became a maid in one of the big sea captains' houses. Her life consisted of cleaning and cooking and caring for children; of being pushed and kicked when she did not move fast enough for either the mistress of the house or the older children. She was spoken to and at as if she did not have any intelligence or feelings.

She slept in an attic bedroom with two other young women and froze in the winter and could barely breathe in the heat of the summer. Being a dutiful daughter, Sarah sent her meagre wages home to her mother to help her and the other children.

Only the thought of being married to Ernest when he finished his degree kept her going. He would save her from this fate of being a domestic and being treated like this. Maybe he would come back and become a school teacher and she would be a school teacher's wife.

She kept these thoughts in her head as she worked her fifteen-hour days of drudgery and abuse.

Ernest, meantime, was accepted into Dalhousie University in Halifax, where he was delighted to meet other students who were like him. He studied hard, wrote excellent essays, passed his exams and forgot all about his promise of marriage to Sarah.

He rarely came home to visit his parents and, when he did, he managed to avoid seeing Sarah as she was in Bridgetown working with only every third Sunday off to see her family. He enjoyed life in the town of Halifax and still looked forward to seeing more of the world.

Sarah heard about Ernest making it home occasionally. She wrote to him at the university and, when he only wrote back occasionally and never mentioned their promise to each other, she assumed it was because he was so very busy with his studies.

One Sunday, when Sarah was home to visit (she could only stay for an hour or so as it took so long to get up the mountain to the settlement and she had to be back at the house in Bridgetown by 7 pm), her mother casually mentioned that that Ernest Buckler was leaving Dalhousie University as he had completed his degree in Mathematics.

Sarah's heart leapt in her chest. A smile came across her face. Finally! It was happening.

Then Mary carried on with her sentence, saying that Ernest was moving to the big city of Toronto. He had been accepted at a university there and was going to take his degree in Philosophy. "What on earth is he going to do with a fancy degree in philosophy?" her mother asked.

Sarah was stunned. Ernest was not coming back. He was not going to marry her Her life would carry on as a domestic, a maid, who would be treated poorly, for the rest of her life.

She put her head down and tried not to cry.

Ernest was having a wonderful time. The University of Toronto and the city wrapped around it had even more to offer than Halifax did. There were theatres and cafés and smoky taverns where he and his friends puffed cigars, drank spirits and talked about the state of the world.

Occasionally he would receive a letter from Sarah, but they annoyed Ernest. He was busy; he was studying and solving the problems of the world. He did not have the patience to read about the petty shenanigans and gossip of the little settlement on top of the mountain in nowhere, Nova Scotia.

Ernest did not even open the letters, let alone write back. He had no intention of ever returning to the West Dalhousie Settlement. He still had every intention of seeing the world after he finished his degree.

Finally, Ernest graduated and was offered a job in a glass building with elevators. He had an office that overlooked the busy downtown streets of Toronto. His life was becoming everything he had wanted it to be.

Except it was not. The job as an actuary turned out to be boring. Very boring. Ernest was very good at it, but that was why he found it boring. There was no challenge.

Ernest wrote more frequently to his parents now, telling them about his life in Toronto, trying to make it sound better than it actually was. He started to write short stories.

But his stories all seemed to revolve around life in West Dalhousie. He couldn't shake those memories, those experiences out of his soul and they were coming out in his work.

Eventually Ernest met someone in Toronto. He fell in love, deeply, passionately and with all his soul.

But their love for each other had to be a secret affair. They could not celebrate it in public and, in the end, his lover ended it, telling

Ernest to forget about their romance and find someone "normal" with whom he could live his life and for whom he would not have to hide his love.

Ernest was heartbroken. He had been taken to such heights of emotion, only to be cast crashing down onto the cold, dirty, asphalt of the streets of Toronto.

His father was having serious health problems by this time. His mother asked him to come home and visit them, as she feared her husband was dying.

Ernest, nursing his broken heart, came home to see his parents and the family farm. He felt he could use the rest. His employer, who liked him so much, told Ernest they would hold his job open for him to return even though it was the height of the Great Depression.

Ernest packed his books and papers and headed back to the family farm on the settlement. It became quickly apparent that his parents needed him on the farm and Ernest, still carrying his wounded heart, decided that he would stay here and care for his parents, at least until they passed.

His Uncle Wallace was disappointed in his decision but understood and helped him out on the farm.

When the position of school teacher became available at his old one-room schoolhouse, perched on the great slab of white granite, Ernest applied for it and got it. He reluctantly let his position in Toronto go. He could not go back to that city and the heartbreak it still held for him.

When the Second World War broke out, Ernest could not go. As a farmer and a schoolteacher who was taking care of his elderly parents, he was considered vital to the home front and told to stay home in Nova Scotia. Ernest was heartbroken again at the thought of not being able to go to Europe and see all the things that his uncle Wallace had seen.

Uncle Wallace came to visit. They took mugs of tea and sat on the kitchen-porch steps, looking out at the world. They pushed a bit of small talk back and forth, but Ernest could tell that his uncle had something he was struggling to say.

Finally, Uncle Wallace drew a deep breath and said, "Europe. I filled your head with such nonsense,"

"You said Europe was beautiful."

"Yes, Europe can be beautiful. But that beauty came at a price. We lived knee-deep in mud, cold, hungry and bored almost to death most of the time. And when we were not bored, we saw things that were so horrible I still see them in my nightmares. Bombs, mustard gas, comrades slowly dying and crying out for their mothers. And there was not a damn thing you could do for them. Being helpless and in a rage stays with you for the rest of your life."

Ernest stared at him. "You never said any of this before."

Uncle Wallace shook his head, as if he was trying to shake memories away from himself. "I told you the exciting parts about Paris and London and Milan to try to block out my darker memories. I did not want you to think that I was a crybaby and could not handle what the Great War did to me. To us all."

Part of Ernest knew that Uncle Wallace was right and that he was lucky not sent to face the horrors of war. But part of him clung to his childhood dreams of the great cities of Europe, of the cafés full of writers and poets and artists.

"You are doing what any responsible son would do," Uncle Wallace said. "You are staying here to take care of your mother and the farm, now that your dad has died."

They sat in silence for a while. Then Ernest said, "I have been writing some stories about the settlement. I know that some people think that living here must be wonderful, so I have written some stories about it. I guess I am trying to see what they see."

"It is wonderful to live here," Uncle Wallace said. "We have fresh air and family. We have a close-knit community with our church. And no bullets are flying past our heads. Many city people envy what we have."

They watched a neighbour guiding his team of slow, patient, powerful oxen along the dirt road on the way to some farm task. They watched a couple of crows playing above the trees.

Finally, Uncle Wallace set down his mug and worked himself to his feet. He looked down at Ernest, then tapped his shoulder. "Those stories. Why don't you send them off to some of those magazines you read and see what they say about them?"

Ernest finally accepted that he was here, in West Dalhousie, and he was staying here. No romance, no jobs, no wars could get him out of here. He would not be travelling the world and he must learn to accept this and make the best of it.

He began to send his stories off to magazines and, to his delight, some were published. Small cheques began to show up in his mailbox. But it was not easy to share his delight in these achievements, as any kind of work that did not involve physical labour was looked upon as an oddity in the community.

Many days were lonely for Ernest. The bookmobile and the rural route mail delivery were the only things that kept his sanity, he felt. He no longer taught at the school house, spending his time tending to the family farm, taking care of his mother and writing about life in such a rural area.

One evening, Ernest was invited to join the men over at Harold Durling's barn. Ernest knew that it would probably end up as an evening of too much hard cider, ribald stories and maybe even a fist fight, but he felt just desperate enough for company that he decided he would go.

As he walked up the road to the Durlings', a beautiful car drew past him and came to a stop a little way ahead. An equally elegant woman emerged. Ernest watched carefully, wondering who she was, why someone like this woman would be visiting the Durlings - or anyone - in this little settlement.

The woman turned and saw him. "Ernest!" she exclaimed with delight. "How lovely to see you! It's been far too many years."

Ernest, still wearing his farming dungarees and boots, felt under-dressed and awkward around this well dressed vision of elegance. Then he looked closer. It was Sarah!

He sputtered her name in shock. "Sarah? Is that you? What are you...? Why are you...? What happened to you?"

Sarah laughed a chuckle of delight. She put her gloved hand in his. The leather felt like butter. The wool of her coat was as smooth as glass and looked as soft as a pillow.

"This is my niece's house," she said. "Abigail Durling is my niece and I am here to visit her for a few days."

"I didn't know you had a niece still living here," he said. "I heard that you left your job in Bridgetown and moved away. That was the last I heard of you."

"I did leave," she said. "Oh, those were hard years. I worked and sent money to mother until the others were grown up enough to take care of themselves and mother. Mother died shortly after that. I left Bridgetown and moved to Halifax. I got a job as a shop girl but I took typing classes at night. I became a typist. And when the war broke out, I volunteered. As I did not have any husband or children, they picked me right away and sent me overseas to Europe."

Ernest could feel his face draining of colour. Oblivious, Sarah talked on.

"Oh, the sights of Europe," she exclaimed. The war was awful, but I got to see so much. I was so good at being a typist that eventually they trained me to be a code breaker. I had security clearances and I associated with terribly important people throughout Europe—generals and politicians and royalty. I was fêted and dined for my skills and knowledge. And, oh, Ernest..." She leaned into him. "I had the most amazing love affairs. But don't tell my niece."

She laughed with delight and happiness. "After the war, I moved to Montreal and learned to speak French. La vie est merveilleuse, êtes-vous d'accord? I married a man named Oscar and we own several small businesses in Montreal.

She slapped him lightly on the arm. "And to think, if you hadn't broken your promise of marrying me, I would have been stuck here, in this little settlement, raising snot-nosed little babies and mucking out cow barns. So what have you been up to these past 30 years? Tell me everything."

Ernest turned and walked away. He put his head down and tried not to cry.

from his intimate acquaintance with "The Car." He has taken science to himself and great things are expected of him. Almost a stranger on the campus, John, however, is known by his singing to all Glee Club audiences.

ERNEST REDMOND BUCKLER

Ernest is first and foremost a brilliant student. He achieved his "A" at the age "when God and games divide the heart" and has since gained several scholarships. He has taken numerous classes in Philosophy and H. E. Taylor had better guard well his laurels. Quiet and unassuming, he possesses a pleasing personality and lacks neither male nor female admirers.

JOHN HENRY BUDD

Johnny can make a piano *talk*, and is responsible for many a wonderful dance, successful Glee Club Show, and "best yet" class party. His side-bowler is Freddy McLellan with his saxaphone, and they both wore out Miss Lowe's front door mat last year. Winner of the Campbell

From Ernest Buckler's high school graduation album.

Brenda J. Thompson

The Gypsies of West Dalhousie

She picked up the rotary-dial phone and dialed the four numbers of Shirley's extension. One short and two long rings and Shirley picked up the party line.

"Hullo."

"Shirley! You have got to see this! Land o' Goshen, they's gypsies comin' up the Morse Road!!"

"Myrtle, are you putting Harold's hooch in your tea cup again? Gypsies don't live in this part of the world!"

Myrtle could hear a snicker on the line; someone else was listening in. Gosh darn, these party lines don't give anyone any private conversations.

"Shirley, I do not drink Harold's hooch. I have told you that many times. It gives me indigestion. I'm tellin' ya, there is a band of gypsies comin' up the mountain! They's comin' up yer way. Yer gonna see them in about ten minutes at the rate they is a movin'."

Myrtle heard Shirley snort on the other end of the line.

But then, "Wait, I sees them meself," Annie Hannam cried.

"Annie, get off the phone," Shirley shouted. "This here is a private conversation."

Annie barrelled on. "They've got a van with all sorts of painted colours and signs on it."

"What do the signs say?" Shirley asked.

"Uhh, lemme see...." Annie was clearly pulling back her curtains to get a better look. "They says 'peace' and 'love' and 'no more ears'."

"What?? No more ears?" Shirley and Myrtle both said at the same time.

"Oh, wait," said Annie. "Sorry, it reads 'no more wars'."

~

Charlie Durling was sitting on his wood pile, taking a break from splitting wood, sipping a little of the 'shine from his still out back. He took a big swig to quench his thirst and, as he lowered his cup, he saw a most amazing sight.

He stared with his mouth open at a band of colourful young people...wait, some were older...walking and dancing and driving vans and cars that were painted with every bright colour under the sun.

Charlie looked into his cup to make note of which batch he was drinking in case he wanted some more. He took another big swallow and looked at the road again. Yup. They were still there, moving slowly, jingling with bells. The colours were still as bright as ever. Charlie decided he would keep this batch of shine to himself.

~

"I will swear on the bible that I saw George Buckler's grandson, Joseph, with that crowd of gypsies," Shirley said as she watched the procession out her kitchen window. By golly, Myrtle was right. There was an army of gypsies moving up the Morse road toward Dalhousie Settlement.

"Joey Buckler moved away to Tarana two years ago," Annie said, stating what they all knew.

"I heard he was attending some college up there. Can't remember the name of it" Shirley responded.

116

"It was something like Rockdale," Myrtle said. "Let me think on it....oh yeah, it was Rochdale."

"Well if he is supposed to be at this fancy college, what's he doing, dressed like he's homeless, in with that buncha gypsies?" Shirley asked. "Why, his hair is so long he looks like a girl!"

"Maybe he dropped out," Annie offered. "His grandfather is gonna be upset after paying good money to get him an education."

They clucked their tongues in unison. Wait until the rest of the settlement sees this.

~

The elders and concerned citizens of West Dalhousie called a meeting at the school house. People from all the churches attended to talk about these gypsies who had taken up camping on George Buckler's land, with his blessing!

"One of those young women was in the store the other day and noticed my wife is expecting." Caleb Spurr said. "She told my wife that her 'community' was having a 'womb workshop', if she would like to attend. I told Mary that there was no way I was letting her go near any such weird people. They sound like a buncha commies for heaven's sake, with the way they talk about sharing and loving and how they don't work for the man. 'What man?' I ask. No one round here would hire them bunch a dirty long haired people."

People murmured and nodded their heads in agreement.

"They are not gypsies," George Buckler told the group. "They call themselves hippies. And they believe in peace and love and sharing."

"Hippies? Why on God's green earth do they call themselves hippies?" Albert Spurr asked incredulously.

"My grandson says it's from the African Wolof word 'hipi', which means 'to open your eyes' or 'become aware'," George answered.

A couple of people snorted in laughter. "They don't look like no Africans," one of them said.

"Become aware of what?" asked another person.

"To become aware of love," George answered. "To become aware that we need to all love one another, to get along, to not have wars that kill our young men."

Some people lowered their heads. They agreed with that notion. So many community members in West Dalhousie had lost sons, grandsons, nephews to wars in parts of the world they had never heard of.

"Where did they all come from? someone shouted from the crowd.

"The hippie movement started in a place in California. City of San Francisco and a neighbourhood called Haight Ashbury," George answered. "Least, that's what my grandson told me."

"Why do they hate ashbury?" someone asked. "Is that why they moved here?"

"Californy?? Why did they move all the way here from Californy?" another asked.

"They did not all come from California," George answered. A lot of these hippies come from Toronto. But some of the young men are from the United States because, as you know, they are fighting a war over in Vietnam and a lot of them don't want to fight in a war they don't believe in."

"So they're a bunch a fraidy cats," someone shouted out.

"Now, Henry," Lester said, "even Canada won't get involved in that war. Didn't you hear on the radio that our government in Ottawa offered these young men the chance to come to Canada so they don't have to serve in that war?"

"I don't like it," Henry answered back. "It's a man's duty and privilege to serve and protect his country. And if they don't like that war, fine. But why do they have to dress like that, with men wearing long hair and long dresses?"

"It is what they call their freedom to choose what they do, what they wear, who they love, how they live," George Buckler said.

This got the crowd buzzing. What do you mean, they get to choose? There is no choice. You do what you are supposed to do, according to the bible, according to your elders, according to your neighbours. You dress like you are supposed to, according to the job you have and how much money you have. You marry the girl down the road that you grew up with. You have children and you teach them to work hard, don't spend any money on frivolous things, save for your old age, don't fool around on your spouse (or, at least, don't get caught), attend church every Sunday and don't give your neighbours anything to talk about.

That's been the rules since this settlement was been founded by good, hard-working, God-fearing citizens. And now this bunch of new people are coming here and saying they don't have to follow any of these rules, that they won't follow any of these rules? What was happening to the world??

The crowd dispersed muttering, shaking their heads in disbelief. Some of the people secretly liked what they were hearing about this new group of people, these 'hippies'. Others just hoped these near-naked people camping in the fields would move along quickly so the settlement could get back to normal.

~

The men adjusted their caps and touched their pistols to assure themselves they were protected should any of these crazy hippies go wild on them. The RCMP had educated these police on Reefer Madness: if any of these weirdos went off on them and started getting violent because of The Weed, they were prepared.

At first the constables surrounded the hippie camp, hiding behind trees, stumps and bushes, watching the community in action. Women were breast-feeding their babies, some men and women were pounding nails to build things...but some of them were working naked! Children were running around without clothes, playing in mud puddles, making mud pies and laughing with each other. People were setting up gardens, cooking food, smiling and having a good time. This was definitely a problem.

Damn it! One of the hippies had spotted them! He smiled and waved to them. "Come on out!" he shouted.

The constables touched their pistols again and looked over to their supervisor for direction.

By this time some of the hippies, men and women, were walking toward them, some with their arms opened wide in a gesture of a hug, some with bowls of food. Damn, that food smelled good, almost exotic smelling.

One of the cops involuntarily said, "Yummm, I smell curry".

Their supervisor gestured to them: their cover was blown. The cops stepped out from behind their hiding spots.

"Welcome, gentle men," one of the hippies said. "Please eat with us. Share our meal."

"There'll be none of that," the head cop snarled. "You probably have it laced with marijuana. We'll not be falling for that, you dope fiends." He gestured to the other cops, "Men, toss their camp!"

The cops moved in pairs to the tents and cabins and began ripping blankets off beds, throwing pillows and clothes. They ripped down Grateful Dead posters and knocked over candles, incense and shrines to peace.

The women and men comforted the children who were becoming upset by this. There were more cops than hippies, but, by the end of it all, they came up with less than an ounce of marijuana, mostly because cops pocketed the vast majority of what they had found.

An older hippie, sporting an Afro like a halo and wearing an African dashiki, stepped forward. "I am assuming you have a warrant for searching our buildings and private belongings," he said.

"Who are you?" the head cop asked, looking over this very tall, African-looking man..

"I am known by my African name, Malik," he answered. "But I am also known by my Halifax name, Harold Ruggles, LLB. And unless you come here with a warrant for the purposes of finding a specific object, I suggest that you do not do this again or we shall be forced to take legal measures against you in response."

~

The elders and concerned citizens of the settlement met again. They had to get rid of this bunch of people who didn't believe in following the rules. Getting the police to raid them for drugs didn't work. Not only did it not work, but the lawyer hippie scared the cops right away. That didn't seem right.

Finally, it was decided that the elders, Ed, Henry and Albert, would get together and confront George Buckler personally about moving them hippies off his property. They went by car over to George's homestead to threaten him, not with violence, but with banishment from the community. They liked George and did not want to banish him but he was letting these hippies go too far.

They gathered in the kitchen. George's wife had passed years ago, so George made them some tea himself while they presented their arguments.

George listened to their persuasion and thinly-veiled threats and said very little. Finally, he drained the tea from his cup and said, "Why don't you come and meet my neighbours before you decide that I have to evict them? Perhaps if you got to know them a little better, you might change your minds."

Henry, Ed and Albert discussed it for a bit and then decided that, yes, they would meet the hippies. They were sure it would strengthen their case for getting rid of them.

George led the men along a wooded path toward the field where the hippies were camping. But then he turned off that path, and took them down the path toward the Spurr stillwater.

The elders could hear some of those damn dirty hippies splashing around, laughing and having fun.

"Well, at least some of 'em will be clean" Ed thought to himself.

"Joey!" George shouted to his grandson. "Bring some of your friends here to meet my friends"

Joey straightway came out of the water. Durned if he wasn't naked as the day he was born.

But then Joey's hippie friends started coming out of the water as well. And they were all naked. They were smiling and talking and introduced themselves to the elders.

Alfred didn't hear a darn word they said. He just smiled and hoped he wasn't staring. He had never seen such beauty as the naked body in his life. He had never even seen his wife completely naked. He had never realized what beauty he was missing. And when one of the young women spoke to him, all he could hear in his head was his own voice telling him, "Smile and look her in her eyes, you old goat!"

Henry felt like he couldn't move his facial muscles. He had a deadpan face as the hippies came out of the water and strolled around, naked, and talked with the elders. Women, men, children all naked and acting like this was as natural as nature.

When one of the hippie men took his hand and looked into his eyes, Henry felt himself begin to blush. No one in the Settlement had ever known the real Henry, and all this hippie had to do was look into his eyes.

Ed couldn't manage to sputter out a single word. He just tried to keep his mouth shut and he did it by smiling and shaking the hands of the hippies as they introduced themselves and their children.

The three elder talked for a bit with the hippies then followed George back up the path to his homestead. They said goodbye to George and got into the truck and drove away, down the old military road, back toward the settlement. Nobody said a thing for the first two miles.

Finally Henry spoke up. "They weren't so bad," he said decisively.

"Nope," said Ed, remembering the beauty of the nakedness he has just witnessed.

"Soft," said Henry, almost wistfully. Albert and Ed looked over at him.

"I meant 'gentle'," he corrected himself. "These are gentle people.".

All was quiet in the truck for another two miles.

"I don't have problem with them living here now that I've talked to them," Henry said.

"Nope," Ed agreed.

"I think we need to just let the rest of the community know that they're okay, just different from us," Henry suggested.

"Yup," Ed agreed.

"What about you, Albert?" Ed and Henry asked, turning to him. "What do you think about them hippies staying here?"

"Darn it! I forgot my hat down by the still water," he said. "We'll have to go back."

Ed turned the truck around right away.

The invaders built geodesic domes in West Dalhousie and several other communities in the Valley (this one was in Round Hill).

Agnes and the Monsters

1940s

Agnes gathered her robe around her tighter. The wind was cooler than she had thought.

She walked around the remnants of her summer garden, looking for remaining potatoes or onions she might have missed. She glanced over at the windows of the farm house. The winter curtains would have to go up soon. She lived only in her bedroom and the kitchen when winter set in, but she needed the heavier curtains to keep the cold of the winter out.

"Such a big house for one little old lady" she thought to herself. There was a time when this house was filled with children, with family. Now look at it. Quiet. Lonely. Housing one sad little old lady and falling down around her. The roof was sagging from years of rain and snow and no repairs.

Her grandparents had built their homestead far outside the Dalhousie settlement when it first started, thinking that the settlement would grow to include them someday and they would have a nice plot of acreage to sell to new farmers. Only the settlement did not grow in their direction. Instead they had isolated themselves almost eight kilometres into the woods.

For a long time, it did not matter. Her grandparents had 14 children, 12 of whom survived into adulthood. The two babies who died before they were five years old were buried on the homestead and their little graves were marked with stones that Grandfather

125

chiselled out himself.

They worked hard at building their farm. But the land was rocky and the soil thin and acidic and not conducive to crops. So they raised as much as they could for their own food, and Grandfather purchased some oxen and they commenced a logging business. Grandfather would select the trees for logging and he and his sons would chop them down so the oxen could pull them out to the road.

The trees would be earmarked for buildings in the settlement or taken into the town of Bridgetown, sometimes Annapolis Royal, for ship building. Sometimes the logs were even sent to the United States for ship building down there.

As Grandfather grew older, his son Jacob took over the business more and more. Jacob built a mill right on the homestead and their family prospered. The farmhouse became bigger when Jacob married and had children, one of whom was Agnes' mother, Mildred.

Jacob's brothers mostly moved into the Dalhousie settlement to marry and start families of their own. Some started their own homesteads, others worked for companies, and two even moved to the United States to find jobs and spouses.

Mildred grew up at this old homestead with her grandparents who, when they died, were buried over in the family graveyard next to their children. Some of Agnes' brothers and sisters died when illnesses swept through the settlement and even made it out to them in the woods. The Spanish Flu of 1918 was particularly hard on the settlement and Jacob's family, taking his wife and five of his seven children. They were all buried with much lament and sorrow next to the graves of their grandparents and the babies.

Now Jacob was left with his two remaining daughters, Agnes and Mildred. Agnes knew what she had to do, being the eldest daughter. At the age of 15 she went to the Dalhousie settlement and found the hardest working single man she could find and she proposed to him.

His name was Frank and he knew what was expected of him. He moved with Agnes back to the old homestead in the woods and helped Jacob with the logging and the milling. He and Agnes had two children, John and Millicent.

And life continued.

In 1928 Jacob died and was buried with the other family members in the family graveyard. It was just as well that he died then, as there was this big stock market crash the next year in the United States and, somehow, it affected even little old Dalhousie Settlement. Prices were down and no one had any money for buying wood from the mill.

Then the worst thing of all happened. Late one summer, Jacob and John got a contract for some rough logs. As they were as poor at the homestead as anyone in the village, Frank and Agnes were thrilled to have some money to come in.

Frank and John were gearing up the oxen to take the load of logs to Bridgetown. When they were paid, they were to pick up some flour and oats to get them and their animals through the winter before they headed back home.

Frank and John left together, gee-hawing the oxen to pull the load of logs, early in the morning. Agnes expected them to come back at nightfall or maybe even in the morning. She hummed as she worked in the house, making a hearty meal for when the men returned.

She stopped humming when she heard one of the men from the settlement came running through the woods to the farm.

"Agnes!! Agnes!!! Come quick! There's been an accident!"

Agnes didn't even bother taking off her apron. She left Millicent to tend to the farm animals and ran as fast as she could, following the man through the woods in a shortcut over to the Morse Road.

After running for nearly an hour, she came to the spot where the accident happened. The load of logs on the wagon had somehow become unhitched and the wagon had gotten ahead of the oxen. The logs tumbled off and both Frank and John were killed as the logs rolled over them.

Agnes was devastated. Her husband and son were buried on the homestead with the other family members.

Though numb with grief, Agnes taught herself how to run the mill. Some neighbours, out of sympathy, put some work her way.

But it was just unnatural for a woman to run a mill, they reasoned, and eventually the work dried up.

Another husband was not to be found, either. Agnes was now in her 40s and work-worn. Most men in the settlement were married with their own wives.

Besides, electricity had finally come to the Settlement and people marvelled at what they could do with this new-fangled invention. They had lights to read by in the evenings; things that were once difficult now became easy as more and more contraptions were invented that used this electricity. Radios told them the news from the outside world and men could listen to boxing matches all the way from the United States as it was happening! It was a wondrous thing, this electricity. No one wanted to move to a homestead back in the woods where the electricity did not reach.

Millicent found a job in a hotel in the United States and went there for the summers, bringing her earnings back with her each autumn. This, added to Agnes' widow's allowance, kept the farm and house going for a little while.

Then Millicent found a man. He was from Boston, and when they married, she lived in Boston with him.

For a while Millicent and her husband sent money back to Agnes. But as their children came, the money they could send got less and less, and finally stopped.

Agnes lived in the big farm house by herself, surviving on

her widow's pension, a few chickens and the vegetables she grew in her backyard. "I would rather live on this pittance in a falling-down house then end up in the County Home," she answered when people asked why she still lived there.

Agnes tended carefully for the family burial ground and often found herself talking with the stones, telling them her problems. Sometimes they whispered back to her, words of comfort and encouragement. Agnes made a rare purchase of a frivolous item, a white lilac bush, which she planted next to the graves of her family.

She walked to the Dalhousie Settlement less and less to get supplies for the winter, eventually hiring a man to bring supplies to her. The Dalhousie Settlement grew and waned with the economy, and most people either forgot about Agnes or only heard rumours about her.

When I die, Agnes wrote to Millicent, *I want my body to be buried with my family here on the homestead.*

One day the hired man came by to deliver some flour to Agnes, and found her dead in her favourite chair.

As she requested, Agnes was buried next to her family members on the homestead. Millicent turned her face away from the old, crumbling farm house and returned to her family in Boston.

Many years later, when some big logging company offered Millicent's son money for the land his grandmother had owned up in Canada, he did not hesitate to sell it.

~

2019

The smell of oil and gasoline permeated the air. The vibration from the metal monsters affected even the fish in the brooks. The trees screamed when they were ripped down and dragged across the land where they had grown.

Most local people were disgusted and referred to the clear cuttings as 'moonscapes'. The land looked barren, scary, as if the world we knew was coming to an end and this was what the new world would look like. The new world was called Clear Cutting and everything in the path of the monsters, save one ridiculous little patch of trees, was sheared, ripped, and slashed down. Trees, brush, nests, dens...it did not matter to the Monsters. All of it was to be killed.

The local people had tried hard to convince both their government and the corporations that logging could be done in a different manner, a responsible manner which did not leave the land looking like a war zone with animals, birds and even mushrooms losing their habitats. The governments listened but were politically beholden to the corporations.

In a show of good will, the government held community meetings and round tables, and funded reports to investigate clear-cutting practices. But while these conversations dragged on, the corporations moved their monsters across the land like war tanks in a battle, killing, maiming and destroying everything in their path.

Roger worked for one of these corporations. He did not like what they did; he did not like how they did it. But he needed a job. Both he and his wife worked very hard to keep their family afloat. They had a mortgage to pay, kids to feed; one wanted to go to university and "Lord knows that, in Nova Scotia, the wages were low and the prices were dear," Roger thought to himself. A family could not survive off one wage any more; both the parents had to work and the wages were not going up.

Roger shook his head when he thought about how much his government bragged about keeping the wages down to attract big corporations like the one he was working for. Not only did the corporations keep the government in line with what they wanted, but they didn't even pay taxes. People like Roger and his wife paid the taxes that kept the government going and if the government kept the wages low, then the taxes they paid would be low. Roger couldn't understand why the government couldn't see, wouldn't see the stupidity of that..

Roger was on a conveyance crew that moved ahead of the metal monsters, finding the best path to move them forward. As he cleared brush ahead of him he saw old foundations. Nothing new there, he thought to himself, there were plenty of them in the forests in Nova Scotia.

Rural areas had been depopulated as the economy grew worse and worse with mismanagement and a centralizing of businesses and services in the urban areas. Now the youth moved out west instead of moving to the states, looking for jobs that paid enough for them to live on. Old homesteads were abandoned and left to rot into the ground as families moved out to other provinces to try to survive.

Roger was surprised, however, when he came across an overgrown white lilac bush, a sure sign that someone once lived on this land. But as he cut back the bush, he found that it was concealing headstones that marked the graves of several people. He ran his fingers over the lettering that had faded; they were all from the same family.

Roger said a little prayer over the stones as his boss, Fred, arrived to see what he was doing.

"Look at this." Roger pointed out the stones. "This is a family graveyard."

Fred looked over the stones. "Yeah, And?"

"Well, we should let the government know there is a family burial site here. Then they'll make the company halt the logging around it and save the graves."

Fred looked at Roger like he was crazy. "Do you think the company cares about worn down stones that mark the spots of some mouldering old bodies?"

Fred walked over to the stones and pushed some of them over with his boot. "There! Now we don't see them."

"But—"

"Listen. Do you want a job or not? It pays better than most around here, and if you want to keep it, I suggest you keep your mouth shut. We have a new god now and its name is Greed. Don't get in its path or it will cut you down like these machines cut down these trees."

The mortgage, the price of food, the cost of university all ran through Roger's mind in a flash. He shut his mouth and turned his back.

Fred ordered the monsters to move over the stones and bury them under dirt and greed.

A monster in the West Dalhousie woods in 2019. (Author's photo)

Brenda J. Thompson

Acknowledgements

Writing a book of local stories takes cooperation from many people. I would like to thank those who helped with this book. In particular, I would like to thank the family of Lester Beeler, who generously shared his Memoirs. I wrote a monologue based on Lester's stories for a play for the West Dalhousie Community Hall in 2017. The monologue then played at the Atlantic Fringe Festival in Halifax and the Fundy Fringe Festival in Saint John, and in community halls throughout the Annapolis Valley.

Denise Rice assisted with the background of several stories of the Old Military Road while Jonathan Gillis allowed me to borrow his binder filled with stories from the area. Julie Hannam allowed me to borrow her book of Lord Dalhousie's Journals (I'll bring it back to you, I swear, Julie!) and old newspapers, and the Nova Scotia Archives helped fill in the background of some tales.

Thank you to John and Angela Buckler for reading over the manuscript and correcting technical errors.

Thank you to my editor, Andrew Wetmore and to my cover designer, Rebekah Wetmore.

To my parents, Rick and Juanita (Jess) Thompson for always being supportive,

To my daughters Gwynneth and Megan for not rolling their eyes when I went off on another history rant, and to my husband Kent Folks for tolerating the messiest kitchen table ever.

Thanks to all of you who love, read and support local history.

Brenda J. Thompson

About the author

Brenda J. Thompson has been a local history buff and writer all her life. Plays, short stories, press releases, protest chants, non fiction, fiction...nothing escapes her pen. An anti-poverty activist by nature, writer by choice, Brenda has won awards for her writing.

In 2019, Brenda founded Moose House Publications to provide a platform for writing in and about rural Nova Scotia. As of December, 2023, Moose House has published more than 70 titles, many by first-time authors.

Brenda lives in Perotte, Nova Scotia, not too near to Annapolis Royal.

www.ingramcontent.com/pod-product-compliance
Lightning Source LLC
Chambersburg PA
CBHW071158120626
46546CB00006B/2319